The Henry Ford Museum

The Henry Ford Museum

by

The Henry Ford Museum Staff

Crown Publishers, Inc.   New York

© 1972 by The Edison Institute, Henry Ford Museum, Dearborn, Michigan
All rights reserved. No part of this book may be reproduced
or utilized in any form or by any means, electronic or mechanical,
including photocopying, recording, or by any information storage
and retrieval system, without permission in writing from the Publisher.
Inquiries should be addressed to Crown Publishers, Inc.,
One Park Avenue, New York, N.Y. 10016.
Library of Congress Catalog Card Number: 79-147329
ISBN: 0-517-506793
Printed in the United States of America
Published simultaneously in Canada by General Publishing Company Limited
10 9 8 7 6 5 4 3

Contents

Greenfield Village and Henry Ford Museum: "Unity with the Past"
  Preface by Frank Caddy, President 6

Henry Ford Museum
  Introduction by Robert G. Wheeler, Vice-President, Research and Interpretation 8

    I. Decorative Arts Galleries 14
      1. Furniture 14
      2. Clocks 30
      3. Metals 32
      4. Painting and Sculpture 38
      5. Ceramics 42
      6. Presidential China 46
      7. Glass 48

    II. Street of Shops and the Folk Art Collection 52
    III. Mechanical Arts Hall 72
      1. Agriculture 74
      2. Domestic Arts 78
      3. Lighting 80
      4. Power 86
      5. Machinery 90
      6. Communications 92
      7. Transportation 100

    IV. Special Exhibitions 128
    V. American Drama Festival 134
    VI. Educational Activities 136
    VII. Museum Research Library 138
    VIII. Ford Archives 142

Index 147
Contributing Staff for This Publication 152

Greenfield Village and Henry Ford Museum: "Unity with the Past"

Preface by Frank Caddy, President

Shortly after Greenfield Village and Henry Ford Museum were dedicated, founder Henry Ford succinctly stated their purpose: "to give us a sense of unity with our people through the generations, and to convey the inspiration of American genius to our youth...." In the intervening years, it has been the aim of a dedicated staff to fulfill that promise.

The Edison Institute, which is the corporate name of Greenfield Village and Henry Ford Museum, was founded by Henry Ford, his wife Clara, and their son Edsel and was named in honor of Mr. Ford's great friend, Thomas Alva Edison. It is chartered as a Michigan non-profit, educational institution and is not a part of the Ford Motor Company or the Ford Foundation.

Greenfield Village is spread over 240 acres and re-creates a pastoral setting of early America. Of the more than one hundred buildings in the Village, most are historic structures that were moved here from various parts of the United States. Some, indeed, came from as far away as England and represent the type of home that many of our very early settlers left when they moved their families to the New World.

One of the most significant buildings is Thomas Alva Edison's Menlo Park Laboratory, which has been restored to look just as it did at the time of the invention of the incandescent lamp on October 21, 1879. When Mr. Edison first saw it at the time of the dedication in 1929, he pronounced it "99% perfect." Dismayed, Mr. Ford asked, "What's wrong?" To which Mr. Edison replied, "We never kept it this clean!"

The front entrance of Henry Ford Museum is an exact duplicate of Independence Hall, a fitting symbol of America's heritage. Behind this façade are fourteen acres of objects Americans made and used. In the beautiful Decorative Arts Galleries may be seen incomparable collections of furniture, ceramics, glass, silver, and pewter. Along the Street of Shops are stores of an earlier day stocked with the items their proprietors would have sold. The eight-acre Hall of Technology contains unmatched collections of agricultural equipment, communications, home arts, lighting, power, and the world-famous transportation collection that includes airplanes, bicycles, buggies, cars, and trains. All together, these superb collections trace three hundred years of American industrial history.

Edsel, Clara, and Henry Ford in front of Martha-Mary Chapel, Greenfield Village.

Special events at Greenfield Village commemorate America's past all through the year, every year. In the spring a special celebration evokes memories of the Country Fairs of yesteryear. In June the Muzzle Loaders Festival recalls the Civil War era and, on the Fourth of July, the Let Freedom Ring ceremony on the front steps of our exact replica of Independence Hall re-creates the birth of our country. Then, in early September, there is the Old Car Festival with some three hundred vintage

In Greenfield Village visitors see the substance and settings of three centuries of American life.

Henry Ford Museum offers the chance to study objects of the past.

cars running under their own power. The next month, early celebrations of the end of the harvest season are re-created during our Autumn Harvest Weekend. Christmas is a special time with old-fashioned decorations and displays in both the Village and Museum.

As a nonprofit educational institution, an important part of our program is our service to the community. Annually, more than a quarter-million schoolchildren come to the Village and Museum to learn about their American heritage. In addition, thousands of adults enroll each year in the Adult Education Program. Many of them come from the ranks of the Friends of Greenfield Village and Henry Ford Museum, an organization that is growing in size each year as more companies and individuals contribute funds to further our educational and historic aims.

Americans of all ages, as well as visitors from foreign shores, are always welcome to share with us the richness that is America's heritage. The Village and Museum are open year round and I hope that you'll come and enjoy them with us!

World-famous guests at the dedication of Greenfield Village and the Henry Ford Museum on October 21, 1929, gathered in the entrance galleries of the Museum building at 6:15 P.M. for a formal banquet, with Owen D. Young as Toastmaster. The chambers in which they were seated were lighted by candles. Buildings in the nearby Village were illuminated by gas. Graham McNamee broadcast the proceedings.

Thomas Alva Edison, guest of honor on this momentous occasion, left the dinner and was driven in a horse-drawn carriage to his Menlo Park Laboratory, painstakingly removed from its original site in New Jersey for preservation at Greenfield Village. Here, in the presence of President Herbert Hoover and Henry Ford, he re-enacted that great moment when he, fifty years earlier, had lighted his first electric lamp. Immediately, the Museum's crystal chandeliers blazed with electric light, as did the Village houses. All across the nation and indeed, throughout the world, darkened houses were lighted. This was the moment of Light's Golden Jubilee!

At the entrance to the Museum, enclosed in glass, is a cornerstone, dedicated one year earlier, on September 27, 1928. To symbolize the union of agriculture and industry, Mr. Edison had thrust Luther Burbank's spade into the wet cement, imprinted his own footsteps, and inscribed his name and the date.

The Henry Ford Museum is composed of three distinct areas under one roof. At the front, housed in exact reproductions of Philadelphia's Independence Hall, Carpenter's Hall, and the Old City Hall, are the American Decorative Arts Galleries. Here, superb collections of furniture, ceramics, glass, pewter, silver, and textiles illustrate the development and use of the decorative arts in America from the Pilgrim period to the late nineteenth century.

Henry Ford Museum

**Introduction by
Robert G. Wheeler,
Vice-President,
Research and Interpretation**

Thomas Alva Edison and Henry Ford at the laying of the cornerstone for the Henry Ford Museum, September 27, 1928.

Entrance to the Museum is through an exact replica of Independence Hall. One of the most treasured pieces in the Decorative Arts Galleries is the original Speaker's chair carved by Thomas Affleck (1740-1795) and used in that historic structure.

Painting by Irving Bacon of the banquet held on October 21, 1929, celebrating the fiftieth anniversary of Edison's creation of the incandescent lamp.

Behind is the great Mechanical Arts Hall with its collections—agriculture, home arts and crafts, industrial machinery, steam and electric power, lighting, communication, and transportation.

Uniting these two units is the Street of Early American Shops, where twenty-two buildings stocked with appropriate period collections represent America's eighteenth- and nineteenth-century craft shops and stores.

It could well be said that the Mechanical Arts Hall contains the tools with which America's artisans and farmers worked. The Street of Shops illustrates the surroundings in which so many of them worked with these tools, or sold the products of their hands. In the Decorative Arts Galleries are the products of their labor and the evidences of their daily lives.

Truly, the Henry Ford Museum is a general museum of American history housed in the most American of buildings. Here, with collections matchless in both depth and scope, is the story of America's growth, its inventive genius, the development of its tastes and modes. Any one section of this Museum, be it agriculture, power, transportation, communication, or furniture, is a fascinating history of the American people—their yearnings, their explorations, their accomplishments.

Complementing the collections of the Museum are: a specialized Research Library concentrating upon technical works relating to all the collections, the Ford Archives, a full theater program of America's nineteenth-century drama and of early twentieth-century films, a special exhibitions program, and an Adult Education Program.

Both the Henry Ford Museum and Greenfield Village have individual purposes for being. In the Museum, in unique installations, are the artifacts demonstrating America's movement over a span of three centuries. Little or nothing is missing. The story lines are so complete that they include such diverse elements as telephones, cameras, clocks and watches, refrigerators, stoves, guns, and musical instruments. The in-depth exhibits must be seen to be comprehended.

Greenfield Village with its one hundred structures brought together from many areas of our nation, on the other hand, illustrates in period settings how Americans lived and worked over this period. Nowhere else in the world does such a combination of indoor-outdoor museum complex exist.

12

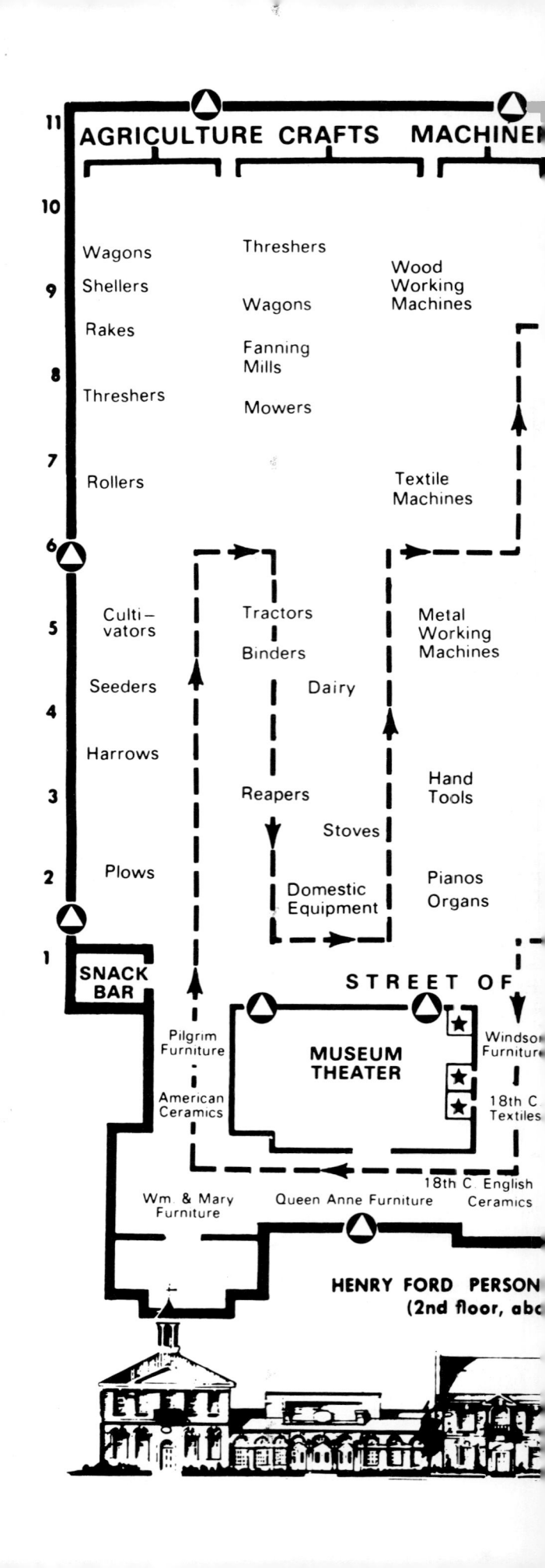

```
11 ─▲──────────────▲─────
   AGRICULTURE  CRAFTS  MACHINE[RY]
10 ┬──────────┬──────────┬
   │          │          │
   Wagons    Threshers   Wood
 9 Shellers              Working
           Wagons        Machines
   Rakes
           Fanning
 8         Mills
   Threshers
           Mowers
 7
   Rollers              Textile
                        Machines
 6 ▲──────────▶────────▶
                              │
   Culti-   Tractors   Metal
 5 vators              Working
           Binders     Machines
                 Dairy
   Seeders
 4
   Harrows
                        Hand
 3         Reapers      Tools
                Stoves
 2 Plows
           Domestic    Pianos
           Equipment   Organs
 1 ▲
   ┌────┐              STREET OF
   │SNACK│        ▲         ▲
   │ BAR │                       ★ Windso[r]
   └────┘  Pilgrim              Furnitur[e]
           Furniture  MUSEUM    ★
                      THEATER      18th C
           American              ★ Textiles
           Ceramics
                              ◀──
           Wm & Mary  Queen Anne  18th C. English
           Furniture  Furniture   Ceramics
                          ▲
                                HENRY FORD PERSON[AL]
                                (2nd floor, abo[ve])
```

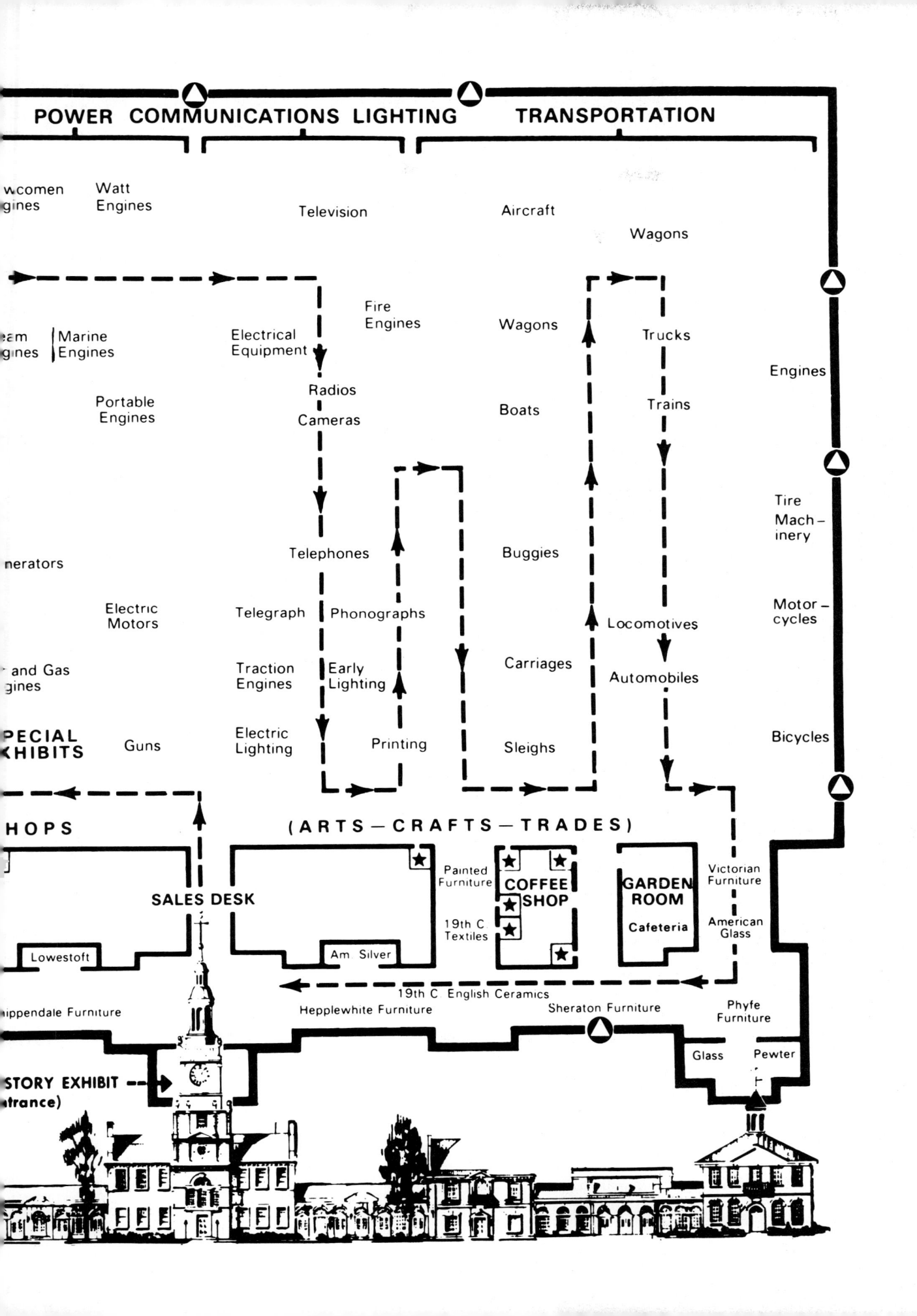

POWER COMMUNICATIONS LIGHTING TRANSPORTATION

wcomen	Watt					
gines	Engines		Television	Aircraft	Wagons	
am	Marine	Electrical	Fire Engines	Wagons	Trucks	Engines
gines	Engines	Equipment				
	Portable Engines		Radios Cameras	Boats	Trains	
nerators	Electric Motors	Telegraph	Telephones Phonographs	Buggies	Locomotives	Tire Machinery
and Gas gines		Traction Engines	Early Lighting	Carriages	Automobiles	Motor-cycles
PECIAL XHIBITS	Guns	Electric Lighting	Printing	Sleighs		Bicycles

(ARTS — CRAFTS — TRADES)

HOPS

SALES DESK

Lowestoft

ippendale Furniture

Painted Furniture

Am. Silver

Hepplewhite Furniture

COFFEE SHOP

19th C. Textiles

19th C. English Ceramics

Sheraton Furniture

GARDEN ROOM

Cafeteria

Victorian Furniture

American Glass

Phyfe Furniture

Glass Pewter

STORY EXHIBIT — trance)

I. Decorative Arts Galleries
1. Furniture

The furniture collections, which include virtually all the existing forms and styles made in America from the seventeenth through the nineteenth centuries, are arranged in the Decorative Arts Galleries as a chronological study collection, interspersed with numerous period room settings. Henry Ford's interest in obtaining objects originally owned by the people who were instrumental in the founding and development of America is demonstrated by the inclusion of many pieces of furniture which personally belonged to George Washington, John Hancock, Benjamin Franklin, Abraham Lincoln, Ulysses S. Grant, and countless others. The products of noted cabinetmakers and of various cabinetmaking centers are also represented.

Left: New England "Carver" armchair, maple and hickory, 1650–1675. Carver chairs are named after seventeenth-century Governor John Carver. This example, with bobbin-turned sloping arms and mushroom-capped front posts, retains much of the original red paint.

Above: The Massachusetts oak, pine, and maple table, with ebonized bobbin-turned stretchers, is typical of the American phase of the Cromwellian style (1680–1700). The half-octagon-shaped Massachusetts Bible box of oak and pine is decorated with carving and dated 1670.

Right: Mary Ball Washington, mother of George Washington, once owned this burl walnut-veneered William and Mary high chest of drawers (1700–1720). It was exhibited at the Chicago World's Fair in 1893, where it sparked a renewal of interest in objects associated with America's past.

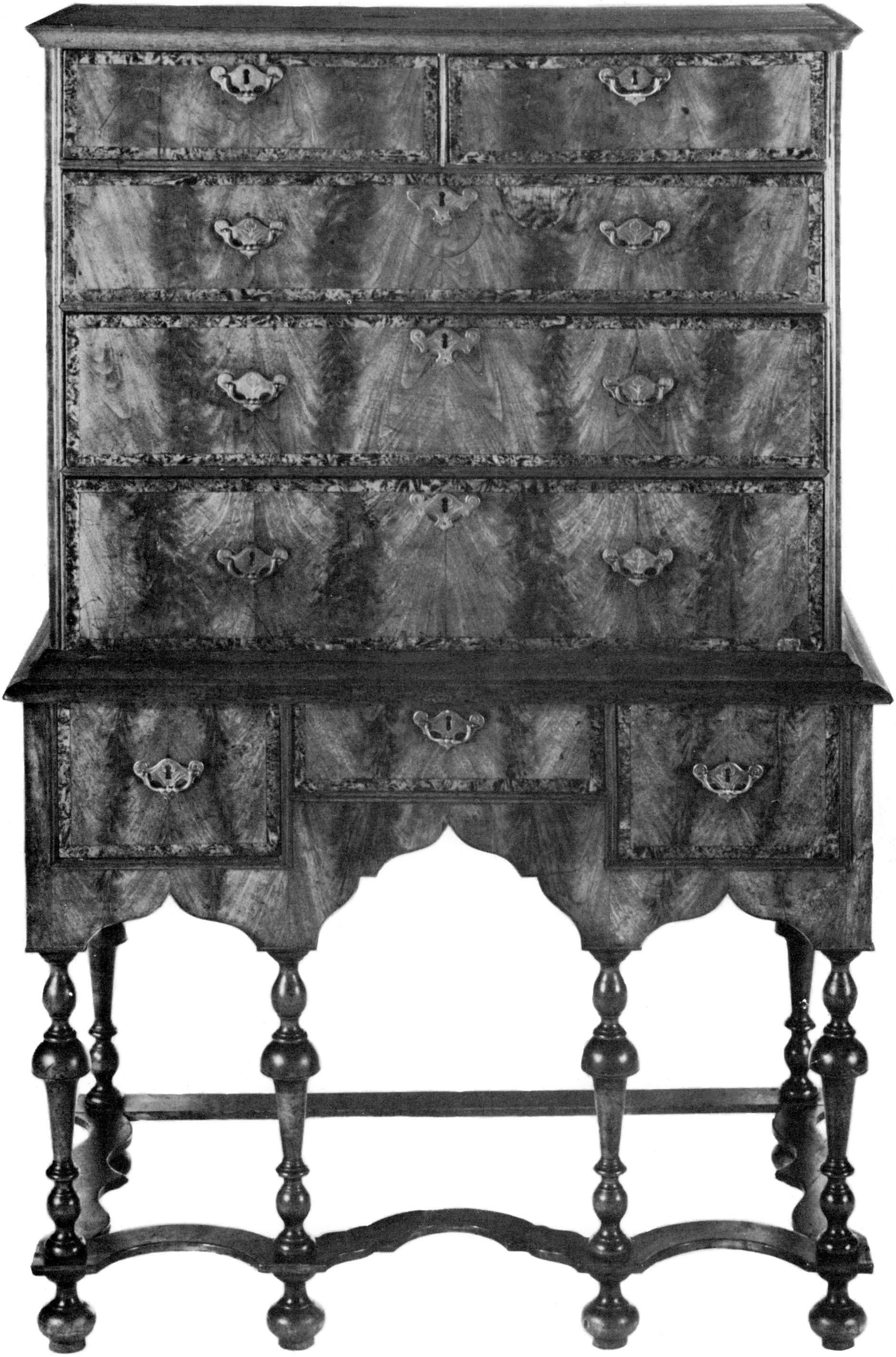

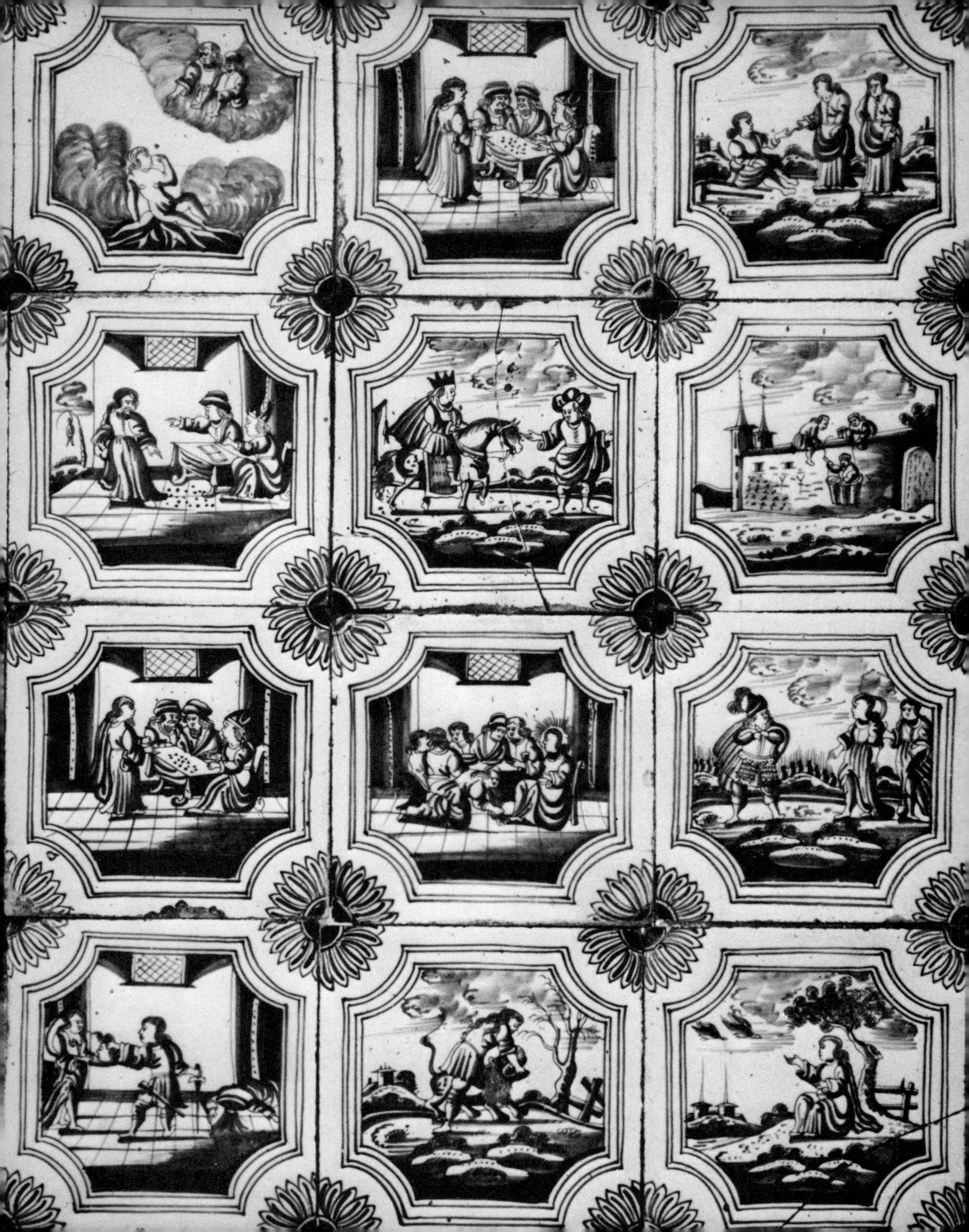

Numerous new design elements were introduced during the American Queen Anne period, 1720–1755. Outstanding characteristics of the Queen Anne style were solid vase-shaped splats in the backs of chairs and cabriole legs usually terminating in pad feet. Although carved shells and arched panels were much used as embellishments, the overall effect was one of simplicity when compared to the more massively proportioned Pilgrim or William and Mary furniture.

Left and Center: The tile-top Queen Anne mixing table with cabriole legs and pad feet, 1720–1740, is the larger of two known. Biblical scenes are depicted on the twenty blue and white Delft tiles set into the top of this unusual piece.

Right: The japanned, scrolled looking glass, 1735–1745, was originally owned by Isaac Van Keuren in New York and probably was decorated by Gerardus Duyckinck, Sr., a well-known artisan of the day.

Below: Solomon Fussell (1700–1762), a cabinetmaker of Philadelphia, Pennsylvania, made this walnut side chair around 1750, one of a pair, for Benjamin Franklin (1706–1790).

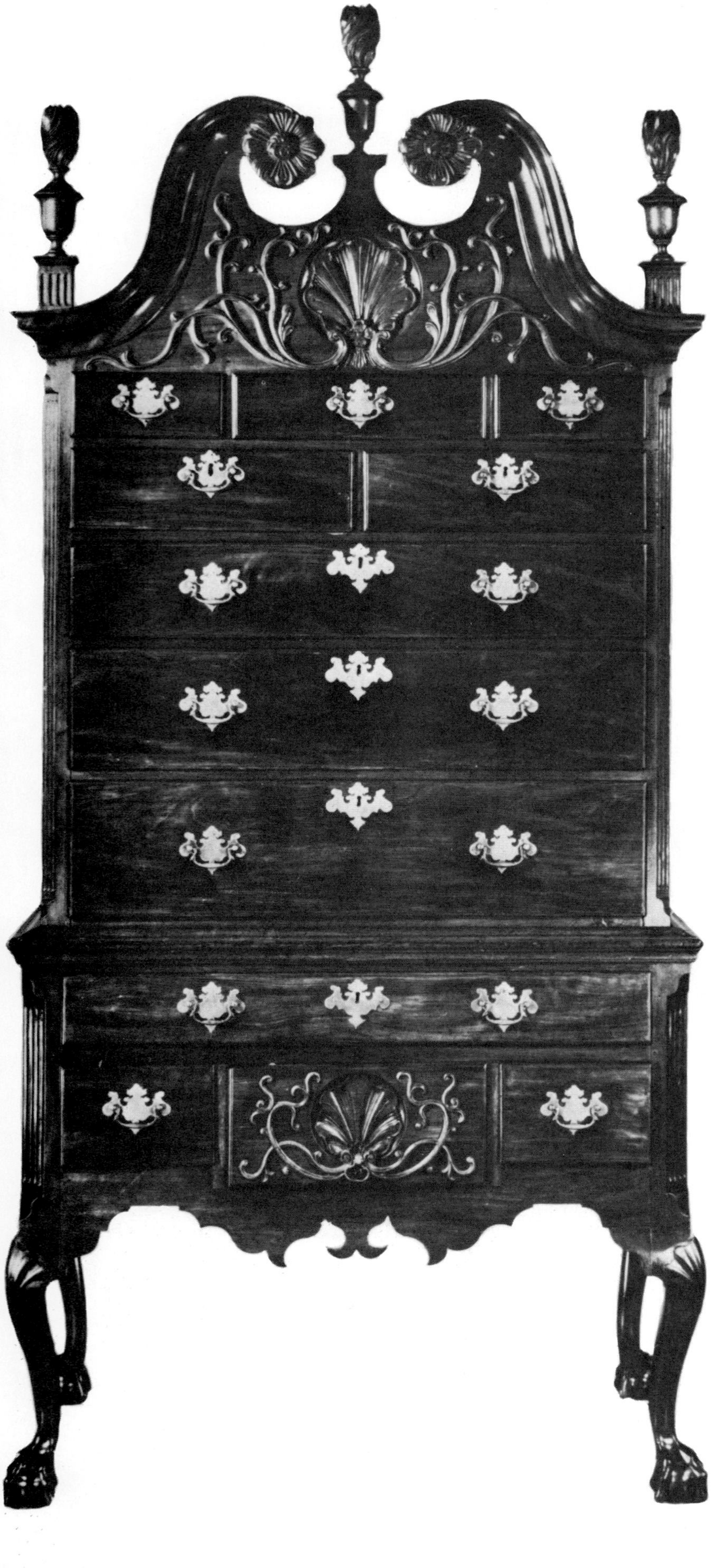

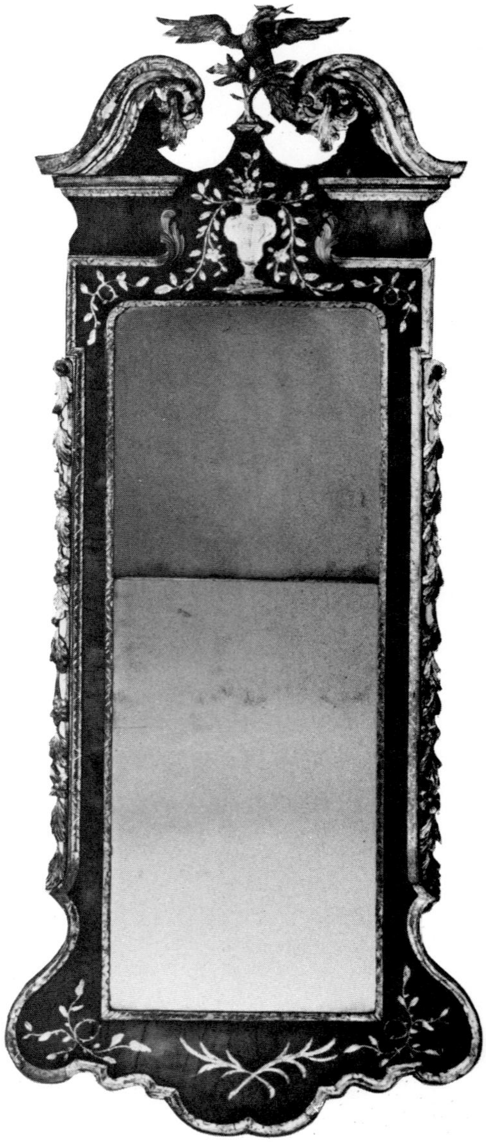

The designs of Thomas Chippendale, a London cabinetmaker, were widely adapted and interpreted by American craftsmen during the last half of the eighteenth century. Characteristic features of the style are cabriole legs with claw and ball feet, carved shells, tendrils and leafage, fluted quarter columns, gadrooning, and the predominant use of richly figured, imported mahogany.

Far left: The elaborately carved mahogany Philadelphia-style high chest of drawers was made in Maryland about 1760.

Center, top: Hosea Dugliss of New York City labeled the walnut, parcel gilded and gesso looking glass, 1798–1820.

Left, below: Of Pennsylvania origin, the mahogany tilt-top table with piecrust edge dates between 1760 and 1780.

Below: The mahogany Chippendale open armchair, with carved eagles at the arms, was made in Massachusetts about 1750.

Federal style furniture, created between 1785 and 1820, expressed the American interpretation of the classical English designs of Robert Adam, George Hepplewhite, Thomas Sheraton, and numerous others. The characteristics of this style are straight lines, the use of inlay and bandings for decorative motifs, and the introduction of a tapered leg and foot.

Below: This leather-upholstered Sheraton armchair is one of a large set made in 1797 by George Bright (1726–1805) for use in the Old State House, Boston, Massachusetts.

Right, bottom: The Hepplewhite mahogany desk with open shelves, circa 1790, is similar to an example used by George Washington in the Federal Hall at New York.

Right, top: The early nineteenth-century bronze, marble, and Wedgwood mantel ornament is topped by figures of George Washington, "Father of His Country," and an eagle, symbolic of infant America.

21

Painting, gilding, and stenciling were popular decorative techniques employed by late eighteenth- and early nineteenth-century craftsmen to enrich their furniture.

Above: The mahogany piano, inlaid with satinwood and brass, is further enhanced with green and gilt stenciling. The case is by Duncan Phyfe (1768–1854) and the works are by Gibson & Davis (working 1801-1820 at New York City).

Below: Made in Baltimore, Maryland, by Thomas Renshaw, the settee and two matching side chairs were decorated by John Barnhart, circa 1815.

Right: Gilded pine girandole mirrors with either concave or convex glasses were popular embellishments of early nineteenth-century homes.

23

Early in the nineteenth century, the Hepplewhite and Sheraton styles evolved into the Empire style.

Below: The couch, carved, circa 1810, in Salem, Massachusetts, by Samuel McIntire (1757–1811), illustrates Grecian influence in the scrolled ends and Roman influence in the flared or saber legs.

Bottom: This Empire room setting exhibits classical furniture forms, several of which were made by the renowned New York cabinetmaker Duncan Phyfe.

Right: Made in Philadelphia by Joseph B. Barry and Sons, circa 1820, the large mahogany veneered breakfront-desk was used by Andrew Jackson at The Hermitage. Classical devices on this piece are the gargoyle figures on the corner columns and the brass animal-paw feet.

25

26

Because the American Victorian period lasted almost sixty years—from 1840 through 1900—there are many substyles which are considered by scholars as movements within themselves. The last phase of the Late Classical Movement during the 1840s was based upon large, simple, scrolled furniture with elegantly veneered or walnut surfaces. The ornate exuberance of the Rococo Revival, popular during the 1850s and early 1860s, contrasts with the quiet restraint of the flat incised carving and inlays of the Renaissance Revival of the 1860s and 1870s.

Left: The New York furniture firm of John Henry Belter (1804–1863) supplied Abraham Lincoln with this elaborate laminated "turtle top" table. It is part of a large suite of parlor furniture used in Lincoln's Springfield, Illinois, home.

Right: Though many critics decried chairs constructed in the Renaissance Revival style as "instruments of torture," they were immensely popular and provided nouveau riche American families with a visual means of displaying their wealth.

Many Germans emigrated from the Old World to America during the eighteenth and early nineteenth centuries in an attempt to secure for themselves the political and religious freedoms permitted in the New World. Settling primarily in southeastern Pennsylvania, they clung tenaciously to the middle-European traditions of their homeland. Whether applied to furniture or pottery, Pennsylvania-German designs are strong and robust. Favorite motifs include the tulip, heart, birds, stars, and other floral and animal forms. The *schrank* or wardrobe *(below)* with its painted and marbelized decoration was made in Lancaster County about 1790. During the nineteenth century, many other European groups seeking religious freedom settled in numerous areas along the frontier. Furniture makers in these settlements produced distinctive styles of their own. A member of the Ohio communal group of Zoarites made, circa 1825, the three-legged walnut table *(center)*. Nineteenth-century Shaker boxes are stacked on it. Furnishings crafted by members of the Shaker sect *(far right, top)* in New Hampshire and New York, as well as in other states, are shown both in the Decorative Arts Galleries and in the Street of Shops.

The most popular chair in America—the Windsor—was used in the humble as well as the more elegant homes of the eighteenth century. Benjamin Franklin signed the Declaration of Independence while sitting in a bow-back Windsor armchair. Thomas Jefferson wrote the historic document on a swivel-based writing-arm Windsor of his own design. During the mid-nineteenth century, simple, inexpensive, painted chairs were confined to rural homes. At first, they were handcrafted; later, they were mass-produced in vast quantities by chairmaking firms who sold and shipped them in wholesale, ready-to-assemble lots. The late eighteenth-century Rhode Island bow-back settee *(lower right)* is a rare Windsor form.

30

2. Clocks

The horological collection consists of over three thousand individual clocks and watches. Elaborate timekeeping devices which also indicate the sign of the zodiac, the solar cycle, and the epact or phases of the moon, dramatically contrast with the ordinary late nineteenth-century kitchen clocks. Most of the outstanding American clockmakers from the eighteenth through the twentieth centuries are represented in this comprehensive collection.

Far left: Japanned tall-case clock. Made by Gawen Brown, Boston, Massachusetts, dated 1766. Eight-day brass movement with hour strike.

Middle left: Tall-case clock in Queen Anne style. Made by Thomas Norton, Rising Sun, Maryland, circa 1790. Steel and brass eight-day movement with brass and pewter dial.

Left, top: Banjo timepiece. Made by Aaron Willard, Boston, Massachusetts, circa 1820. The banjo-style timepiece was invented in 1802 by Aaron's brother, Simon Willard.

Left, bottom: Shelf or dwarf tall-case clock made in 1806 by B. S. Young, while he was a member of the Shaker community at Watervliet, New York. Eight-day brass movement with alarm.

Right, top: Shelf clock. Made by David Wood, Newburyport, Massachusetts, circa 1810. Eight-day brass movement.

Right, center: Pillar and Scroll shelf clock with outside escapement. Made by Eli Terry, Plymouth, Connecticut, circa 1820. Thirty-hour wood movement with hour strike.

Right, bottom: Acorn mantel clock. Made by Forestville Manufacturing Company, Bristol, Connecticut, circa 1848. The picture on the painted tablet is the home of J. C. Brown, president of the company.

Far right: Tall-case clock in Chippendale style. The case was made by Thomas Affleck (died 1795), Philadelphia, Pennsylvania. Robert Shearman made the eight-day brass movement with hour strike. Painted dial.

The silver collection illustrates the changing styles of American craftsmanship from the seventeenth through the revivalistic nineteenth century. Many historic names and events are recorded by pieces in the collection.

Far and lower left: The complete set of James I Apostle spoons, by the unknown maker I. S., London (1617–1618), is known as the Sulhamstead set. The gilded figures that top the spoon handles show the apostolic emblems according to the Germanic system.

Left: The flat-top banded tankard was created by Joseph Lownes, circa 1790, a Philadelphia craftsman.

Below: The custom of drinking tea and coffee provided Colonials with an opportunity for displaying their wealth. Elaborate coffeepots like the example by Joseph Anthony, Jr., circa 1785, the waste bowl by Joseph Richardson, circa 1775, and the covered sugar bowl by William Hollingshead, circa 1780, all Philadelphia craftsmen, were certain to impress neighbors.

Right: The rococo silver coffeepot was made circa 1760 at Boston, Massachusetts, by Paul Revere (1735–1818), the man immortalized in Henry Wadsworth Longfellow's "Paul Revere's Ride."

3. Metals

Because gold is one of the most precious of metals, in America it was usually fashioned into objects of personal decoration rather than into utilitarian pieces. The gold collection is comprised of three major groups—Masonic jewels, mourning jewelry, and decorative adornments. The Museum collection of mourning jewelry, tokens of remembrance given at funerals, is the word's largest and includes several marked rings. Coral and bells (an infant's rattle); a plain gold wedding band given by "Baron" Henry William Stiegel to Elizabeth Holtz during their marriage ceremony in Roxborough, Pennsylvania, on October 24, 1758; and spectacles are some of the more unusual items in the gold collection.

Above: Masonic jewel given in 1855 to Master Samuel L. Fowle of East Boston, Massachusetts.

Near right, top: Masonic jewel marked "T. H.," United States, early nineteenth century.

Near right, center: Masonic jewel elaborately engraved by Francis Shallus, Philadelphia, Pennsylvania, 1812.

Near right, bottom: Group of mourning jewelry from the funeral of Stephen van Rensselaer who died at New York in 1786. The rings are marked by Jacob Boelen II (1733–1786) of New York.

Far right, top: Pair of spectacles by James McAllister, Philadelphia, circa 1840, in their original red leather case.

Far right, bottom: Gold-washed, silver coffee service by Edwin Stebbins & Company, New York, circa 1850.

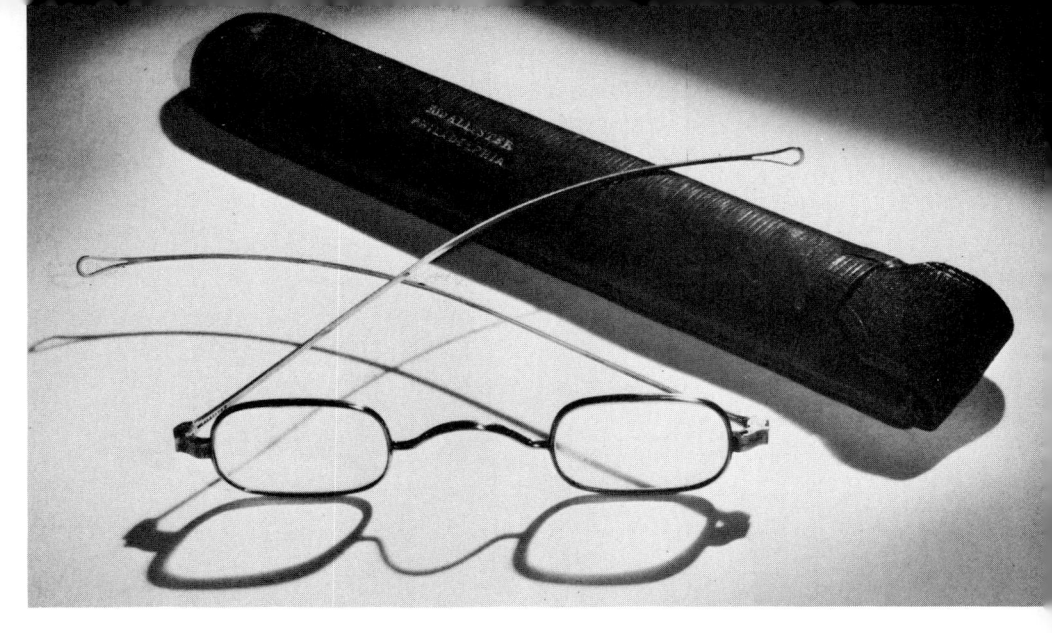

Left: Jewelry originally made for Abigail Matson Coults of Old Lyme, Connecticut, circa 1770. Brooch marked by Ambrose Ward (1735–1809), New Haven, Connecticut.

Objects made from the minor metals, while generally not as sophisticated as those crafted from gold or silver, are equally important in illustrating American history. Unusual examples are the pair of brass andirons and the pewter communion service.

Above: Pewter communion service by Johann Christoph Heyne, Lancaster, Pennsylvania, made for the Canadochly Lutheran Church, York County, Pennsylvania, 1765.

Left, top: Cast iron teakettle, United States, circa 1825.

Left, center: Bell metal skimmer marked by William Barton, New York State, circa 1825.

Bottom: Connecticut River Valley pewter including such makers as the Danforth family *(left case);* Thomas Danforth Boardman and Company *(center case);* Jacob Whitmore, Amos Treadway, Samuel Pierce, Richard Lee, Sr. and Jr., and Ebenezer Southmayd *(right case).*

Below: Brass andirons, Revere-type, Boston, Massachusetts, circa 1780.

Near right: Copper teakettle marked by Best and Russell, Canton, Ohio, circa 1820.

Far right: Decorative wrought iron candle trammel, Pennsylvania-German, circa 1750.

Above: Miniature of James Earle by Robert Field, dated 1802, Annapolis, Maryland. Watercolor on ivory.

Above: Unknown man painted by Joseph Badger, circa 1755, Boston, Massachusetts. Oil on canvas.

4. Painting and Sculpture

Portrait painting—the art of taking a likeness—has been practiced in America since Pilgrim times. Portraits in the collection date from 1700 through the nineteenth century, and were painted by such artists as Gerret Duyckinck, John Watson, John Wollaston, Ralph Earl, Jeremiah Theus, Chester Harding, and many others. The artists represented in a large group of miniature portraits include Edward Greene Malbone, Benjamin Trott, Nathaniel Rogers, Anna Claypoole Peale, Charles Fraser, Thomas Seir Cummings, John Wesley Jarvis, Henry Benbridge, and Thomas Sully.

Center left, top: Miniature of Thomas Ladson Ferguson by Charles Willson Peale, circa 1790, Philadelphia, Pennsylvania. Watercolor on ivory.

Near left, top: Miniature of an unknown man by John Ramage, circa 1780, New York City. Watercolor on ivory.

Far left, bottom: Miss Huysche by Charles Bridges, circa 1735, South Carolina. Oil on canvas.

Above: John Duncan by Thomas McIlworth, circa 1757, New York City. Oil on canvas. Of special interest is the original intricately carved gilt gesso frame on this painting.

Right, bottom: Maria Franklin, first wife of DeWitt Clinton, Governor of New York, by Ezra Ames, circa 1810, Albany, New York. Oil on canavs.

Above: General Henry Dearborn, painted by Gilbert Stuart, circa 1810, New York City. Oil on canvas.

Above: Oil portrait of William Moore signed and dated by Charles Peale Polk, 1797, Baltimore, Maryland.

Near right, top and bottom: Plaster busts of George Washington and Benjamin Franklin by Jean Antoine Houdon, circa 1775, France.

Far right, top: Bronze sculpture, *The Rattlesnake,* by Frederic Remington (1861–1909), cast by the Roman Bronze Works, New York City.

Far right, bottom: Plaster sculpture, *The Council of War* among Grant, Lincoln, and Stanton, by John Rogers, circa 1875, New York City. John Rogers was one of the very first sculptors to sell to the public multiple plaster copies of his original bronzes. Most "Rogers Groups" are three-dimensional depictions similar in effect to the mid-Victorian people and the mid-Victorian scenes that are so frequently the subjects of Currier and Ives prints.

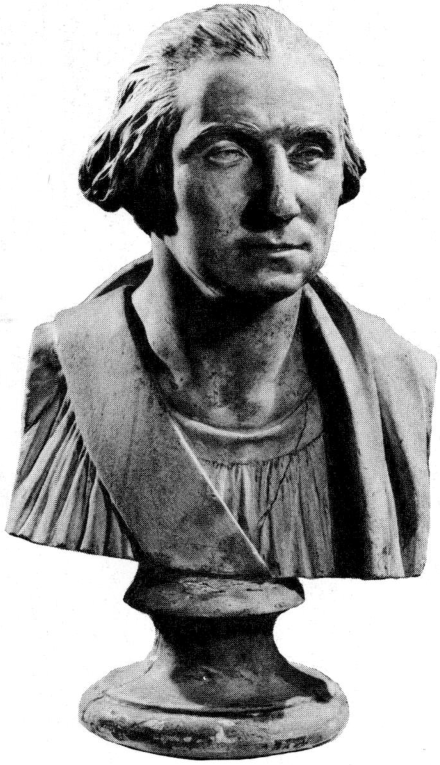

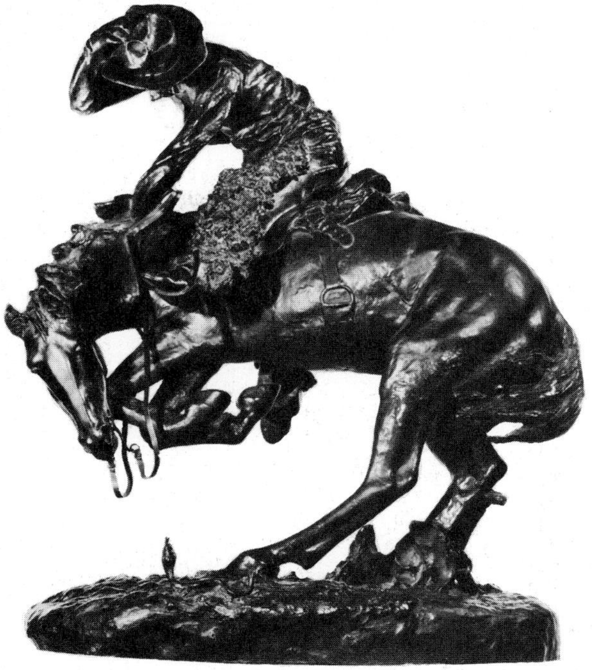

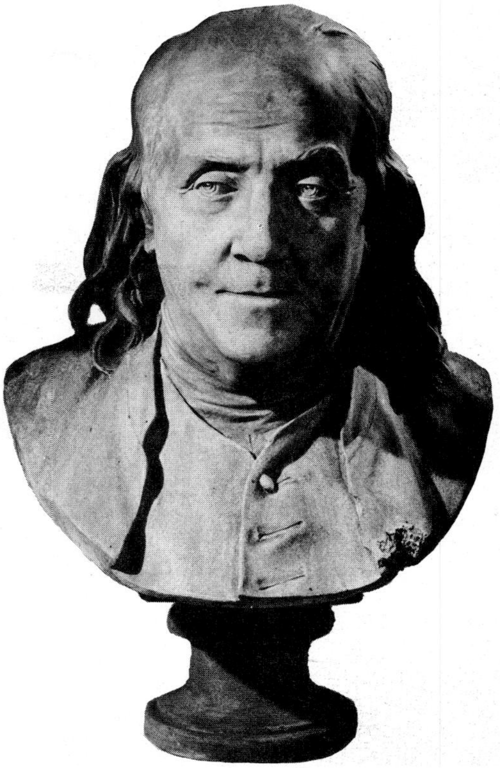

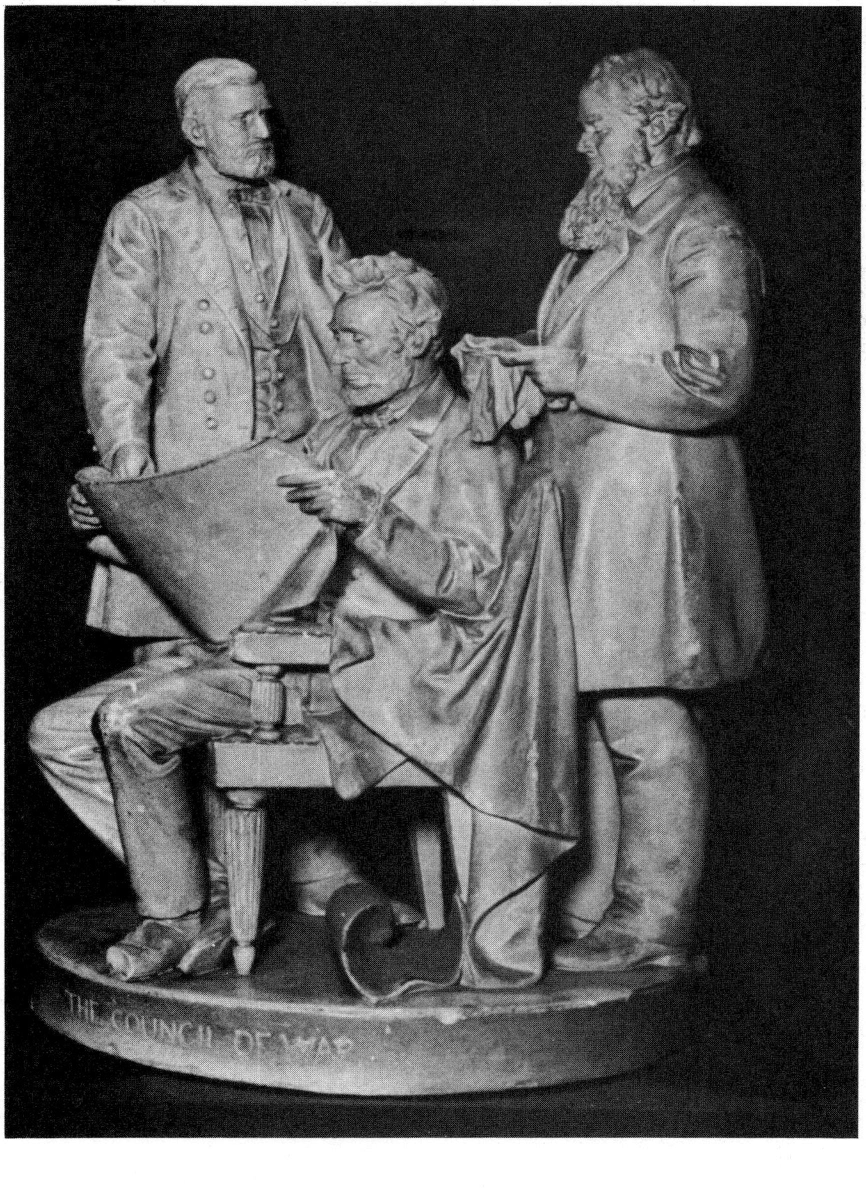
THE COUNCIL OF WAR

42

5. Ceramics

The wives of prosperous colonists who wished to prove their superior position in the community imported their pottery and porcelain from England, the Continent, and the Orient. Makers of American tableware concentrated on functionalism, and their products contrasted sharply with European-made pieces where style and quality were the prime considerations.

Far left: The painted New England Queen Anne corner cupboard, circa 1765, displays examples of English eighteenth-century redware, creamware, Delft, and glass. The types of pottery shown here were listed in an advertisement in the New York *Gazette,* 1771.

Near left, top: The early eighteenth-century salt glaze covered honey jar in the form of a bear is English, and probably was brought to America by an immigrant family or purchased from an Atlantic seaboard merchant.

Near left, bottom: The monumental pistol-handled Chinese export porcelain urn, circa 1785, one of a pair, belonged to the famed Winthrop family of Boston, Massachusetts.

Below: The blue and white soft-paste porcelain pitcher was made at Caughley, Shropshire, England, circa 1775.

Right and below: The shell-shaped teapot with strawberry decoration and the large platter with blue transfer-printed Arms of Pennsylvania were made at Staffordshire, England, about 1825.

Above: The Parian eagle vase was manufactured by the U.S. Pottery Company at Bennington, Vermont, circa 1850.

Right, top: The William Ellis Tucker Factory at Philadelphia produced, circa 1830, the French-style pitcher with landscape scene.

Right: Made by Knowles, Taylor, and Knowles at East Liverpool, Ohio, circa 1890, the "Lotus Ware" Belleek porcelain vase is ornately painted and gilded.

Abigail Adams, wife of the first President to live in the White House, established a tradition when she ordered china for the new Executive Mansion from the French firm of Sèvres. An 1826 Act of Congress decreed that all equipment for the President's House must be native to America when feasible, but it was not until 1917 that Mrs. Woodrow Wilson selected an American firm, Lenox of Trenton, New Jersey, to supply the White House tableware.

Right: An order placed in China by the Society of the Cincinnati for a dinner service as a gift for George Washington was received in 1786. The plate, one of three hundred pieces in the set of porcelain, is centered with the emblem of the Society held by the Angel of Fame and framed with a blue Fitzhugh border. The cup and saucer are a late nineteenth-century English version of the Chinese export service made for Martha Washington. A border of fifteen ovals encloses the names of the states of the Union.

6. Presidential China

Left, bottom: The purple-bordered, gold-trimmed Haviland china State Service ordered by President Lincoln was delivered in 1861. Lincoln demonstrated his respect for the early "buy American" legislation by having his imported china decorated with an appropriate American symbol, the eagle and shield.

Above: Following in the footsteps of his predecessors, Woodrow Wilson and Franklin D. Roosevelt, Harry S. Truman ordered his Presidential China from Lenox. This set was also used by Presidents Eisenhower and Kennedy.

Right, top and bottom: The French, one-thousand-piece Rutherford B. Hayes State Service was decorated, circa 1879, by Theodore Davis with illustrations of American flora and fauna. Mr. Davis's brightly colored service is typical of the flamboyant decorations so greatly admired by Victorian society.

Right, center: The Ulysses S. Grant State Service, made by Haviland & Company at Limoges, France, circa 1870, is decorated with the Coat-of-Arms of the United States and with sprays of native flowers.

47

48

7. Glass

The artistic developments and mechanical improvements of American glass are fully represented in their various regional aspects by the collection of pedigreed pieces shown at the Henry Ford Museum.

Left: The aquamarine, lily-pad-decorated sugar bowl was free blown at the Harrisburg Glass Works, New York, between 1841 and 1843.

Above, left: Frederick Mutzer was responsible for the sunburst-pattern, wisteria sugar bowl which was blown in a three-sectioned mold in New England, circa 1825.

Above, center: The unique, swirled, sixteen-ribbed deep amethyst covered sugar bowl was made by the Mantua Glass Works at Mantua, Ohio, circa 1822.

Above, right: This amethyst flask is from the eighteenth-century glasshouse of Frederick Amelung.

Below: Most of the lacy, pressed, and flint glass in the display case was manufactured by the Boston and Sandwich Glass Company and the New England Glass Company with the aid of a mechanical pressing machine during the second quarter of the nineteenth century.

Above, left: Colorful nineteenth-century whiskey bottles with historic or commemorative designs are one of the many special displays in the Museum's glass gallery.

Above, left: Typical of the ornate glass made to cater to American mid-Victorian taste is the blown honey-amber basket flecked with gold, 1860–1875.

Below, far left: Of special interest is the elegant cut and engraved tableware made in 1858 by his employees for Deming Jarves, founder of the Boston and Sandwich Glass Company.

Below: The purple-blue pressed glass syrup jar in the Lincoln Drape pattern was manufactured at Pittsburgh, Pennsylvania, circa 1865.

Above: The unique collection of glassmaker's tools was used by Ralph Barber of Millville, New Jersey, in making his famed water lily paperweights, circa 1900.

Below: Louis Comfort Tiffany, the American glass master, signed the early twentieth-century three-handled blown vase with simulated antique patina.

51

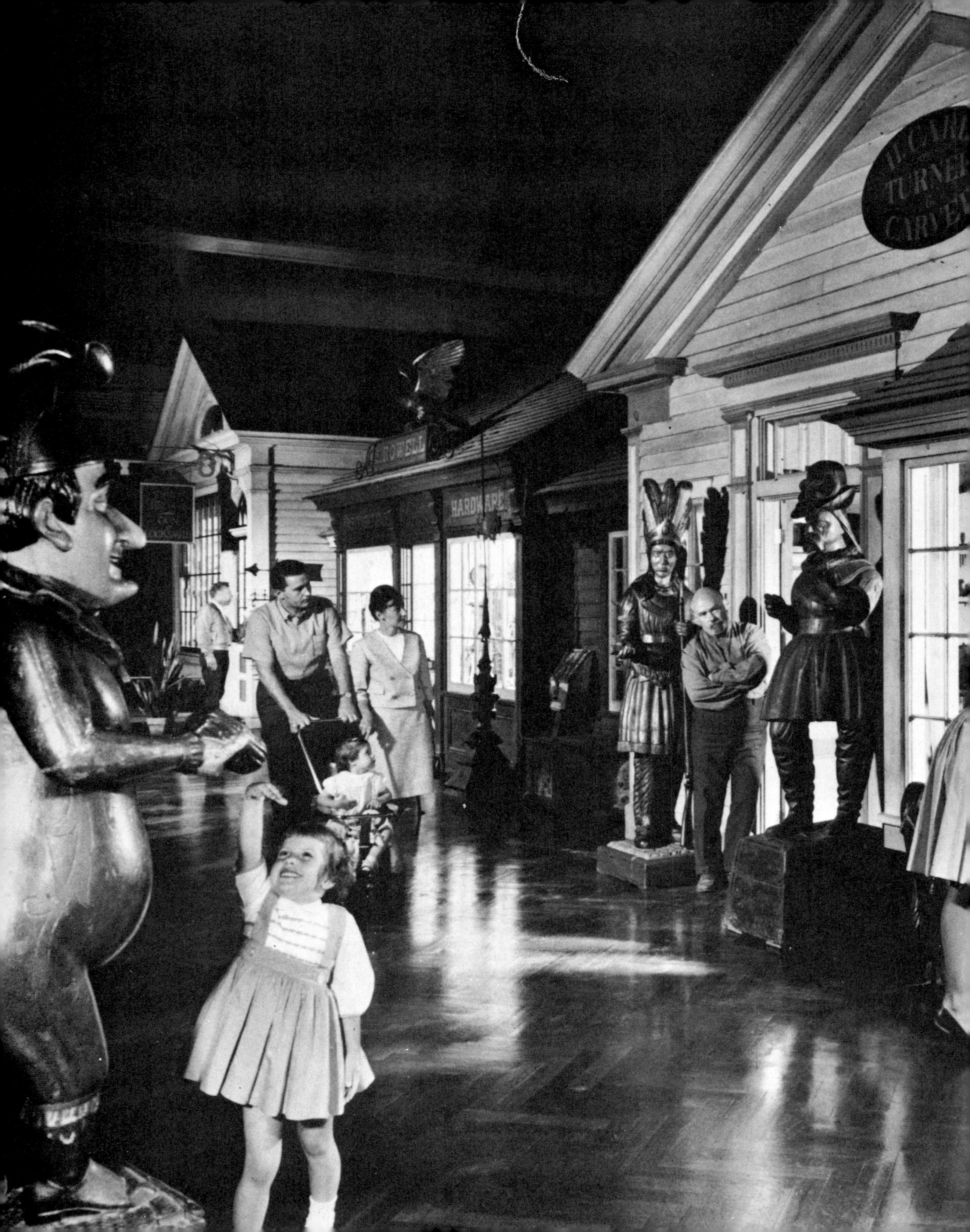
HARDWARE

II. Street of Shops and the Folk Art Collection

Above: Caleb Taft Blacksmith Shop.

The Street of Early American Shops represents handcraftsmanship as it was practiced prior to the Industrial Revolution in America. The twenty-two shops are complete in architectural detail and are stocked with tools, merchandise, and accessories appropriate to their time and purpose. Cigar store Indians, shop figures, and other folk art are picturesque additions to the street. These shops, which were conceived by Edsel Ford, serve as a link between the more formal Decorative Arts Galleries and the Mechanical Arts Hall.

Above and below: Gurdlestone & Son, East India Merchants Shop.

Above and right: Gaily dressed nineteenth-century puppets in *Hadley's Toy Shop* share shelf space with pipsqueaks, pull toys, and carvings by the Pennsylvania-German woodcarvers Wilhelm Schimmel, Aaron Mounts, and John Reber.

Above: Corner Drug Store.

Above and below: Hadley's Toy Shop.

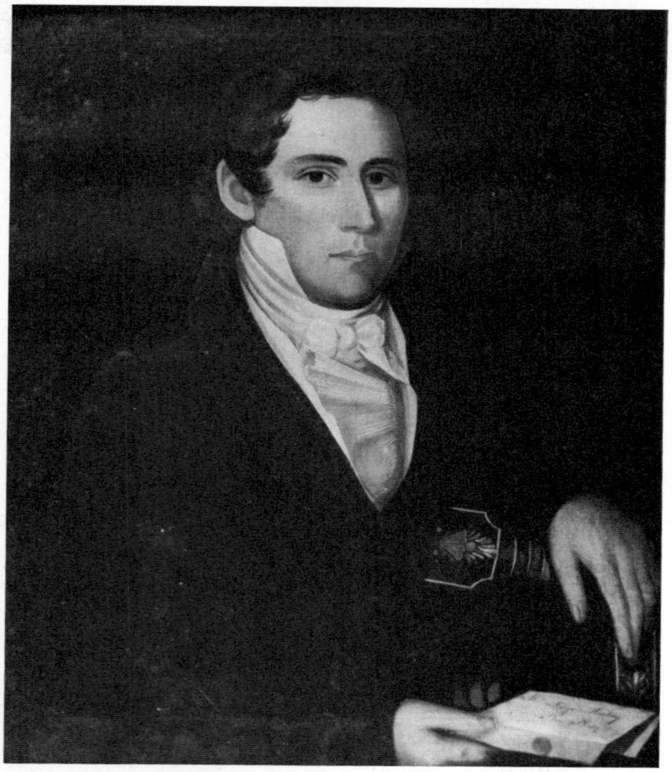

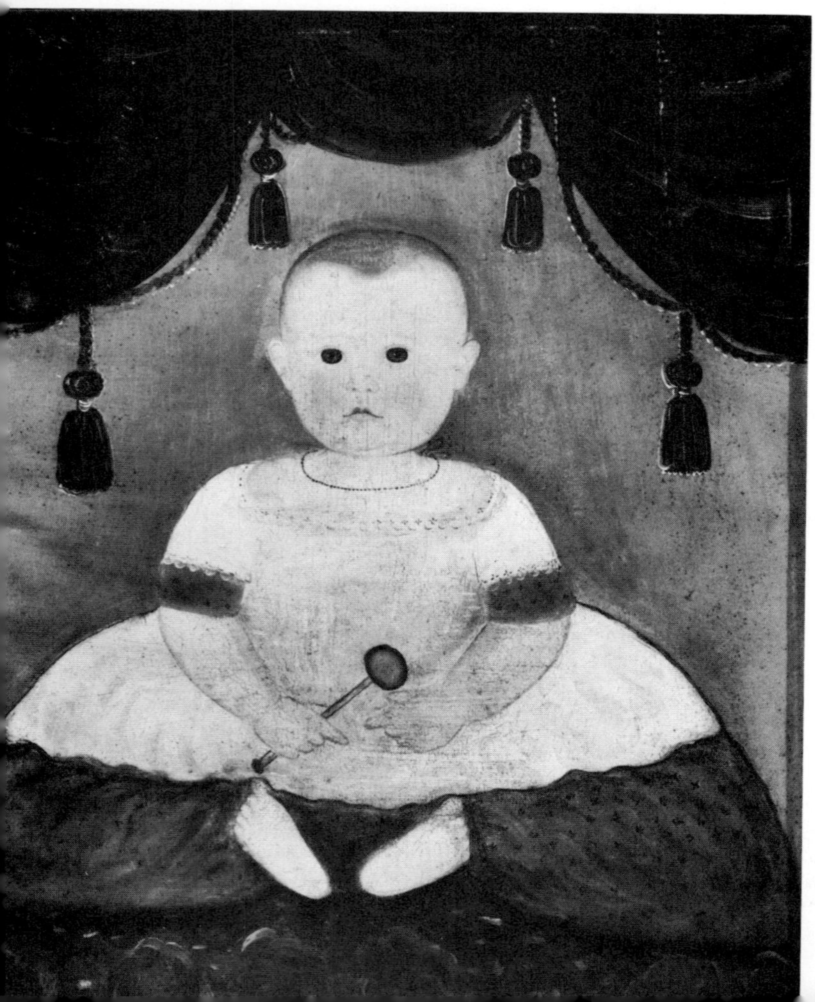

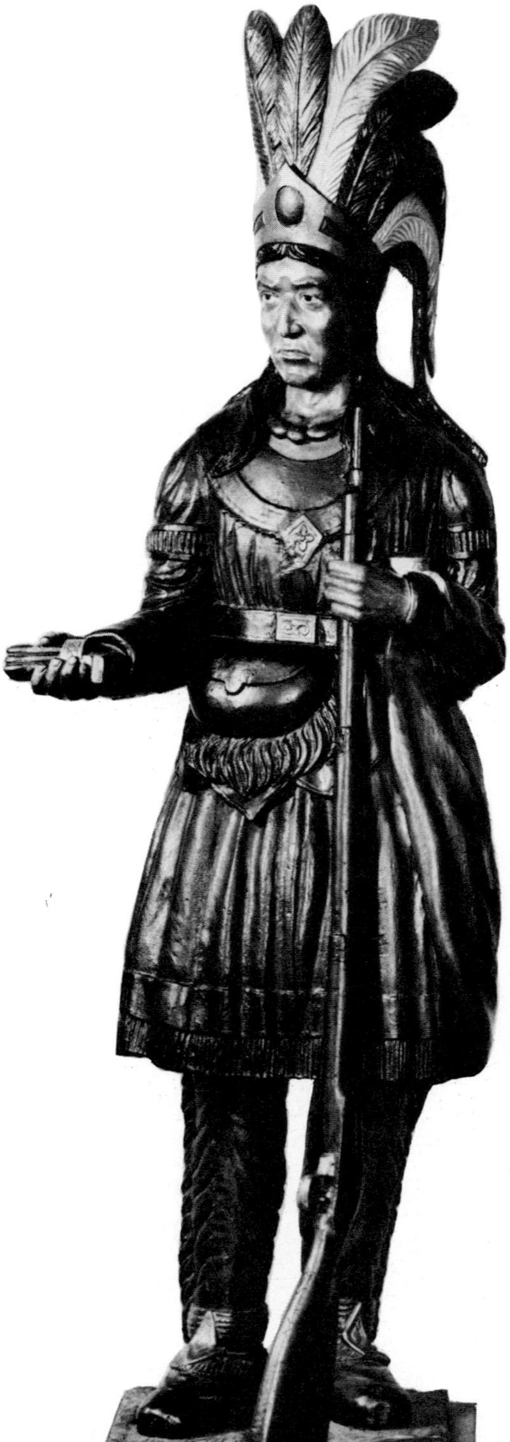

Far left, top: Mr. Morgan Hunting *of Pine Plains, New York, painted by Ammi Phillips, New York, circa 1820.*

Far left, bottom: Unidentified Child *painted by William M. Prior, circa 1845, Boston, Massachusetts.*

Near left: Cigar store Indian Seneca John *carved and painted by Arnold and Peter Ruef, Tiffin, Ohio, circa 1880.*

Right: Girl Coming Through Doorway, *trompe l'oeil painting by George Washington Mark, Greenfield, Massachusetts, circa 1845.*

Below: The Gettysburg Blues *commanded by Colonel C. H. Buehler, Gettysburg, Pennsylvania, painted by an unidentified artist, circa 1845.*

57

Using authentic early American tools and equipment housed in the Street of Shops, Museum and Village craftsmen demonstrate, at various times throughout the year, the arts of cabinetmaking, candlemaking, coopering, dyeing, glassblowing, pewter molding, pottery making, printing, quilting, rug hooking, shingle making, silk reeling, silversmithing, spinning, tinsmithing, tintyping, and weaving. The pewterer *(above, left)* molds spoons, plates, buttons, and miniature toys in the *David Cutler Pewter Shop (below). The* candlemaker *(above),* using beeswax and bayberry, fashions candles in a sixteen-tube metal and wood candle mold. Products from the craft shops are available to Museum visitors.

Above: (Left to right) Quart pewter tankard by William Will, Philadelphia, Pennsylvania, 1764–1798; pint pewter tankard by Frederick Bassett, New York, New York, 1761–1800; rare three-and-one-half pint pewter tankard by Francis Bassett I, New York City, 1715–1740.

Above: Tole document box from the New York–Vermont border area, circa 1825.

Right: Copper weathervane, circa 1875, found in Carlisle, Pennsylvania.

When merchandising their wares, shop owners often used signs painted with illustrations and lettering, or with three-dimensional representations of their products. The *A. Richardson Bootery* sign *(right)* employs both techniques. The interior of the shop *(below)* is stocked with shoes for men, women, and children. The nineteenth-century high-buttoned variety is complemented by a display case of silver and pearl-handled buttonhooks.

Woodcarvings like the dynamic New England polychrome and gilt eagle and serpent *(above)* were created in nineteenth-century shops similar to the *H. Card Turner and Carver Shop (below).*

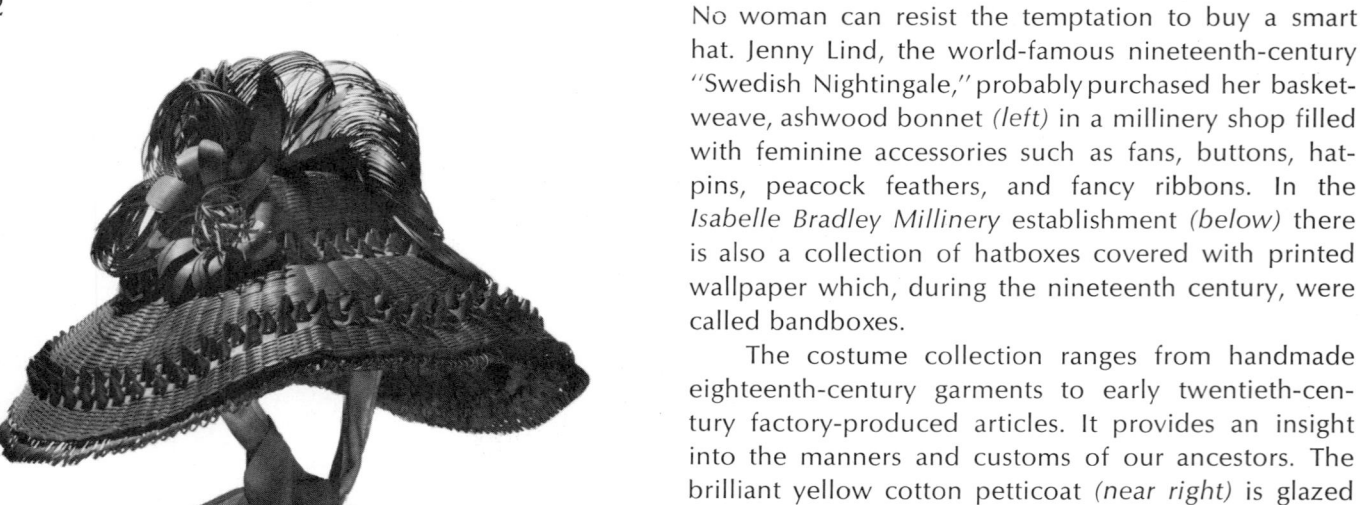

No woman can resist the temptation to buy a smart hat. Jenny Lind, the world-famous nineteenth-century "Swedish Nightingale," probably purchased her basket-weave, ashwood bonnet *(left)* in a millinery shop filled with feminine accessories such as fans, buttons, hatpins, peacock feathers, and fancy ribbons. In the *Isabelle Bradley Millinery* establishment *(below)* there is also a collection of hatboxes covered with printed wallpaper which, during the nineteenth century, were called bandboxes.

The costume collection ranges from handmade eighteenth-century garments to early twentieth-century factory-produced articles. It provides an insight into the manners and customs of our ancestors. The brilliant yellow cotton petticoat *(near right)* is glazed and quilted, and was part of Deborah Read's trousseau when she married Benjamin Franklin in 1730. The child's cotton jacket *(far right)* is printed with portrait busts of George Washington. Coverlets, quilts, and other textiles are occasionally shown in special displays such as the *American Coverlets Exhibition (below)* which featured a loom on which jacquards were woven.

63

Sarah Furman Warner of Greenfield Hill, Connecticut, created an outstanding piece of needlework *(below)*. There is no record of the time consumed by her efforts, but through her precise and intricate design, her superb choice of fabrics for the appliqué, and her meticulous stitches, she created one of the greatest folk art masterpieces of all time.

The silk and cardboard sewing case *(near right)* from Doylestown, Pennsylvania, circa 1800, contains needles, thread, and other sewing equipment which might have been used to stitch the "Pine Tree" quilt *(bottom, center)*. The hand-woven wool, embroidered bedcover with blue wool fringe *(far right)* from New York State is initialed "S.M.B./A.L. 78." Square patterns of conventionalized motifs, embroidered in blue crewels, call to mind the decorative blue and white Delft tiles used around fireplaces in the Dutch-style homes of New Amsterdam.

64

65

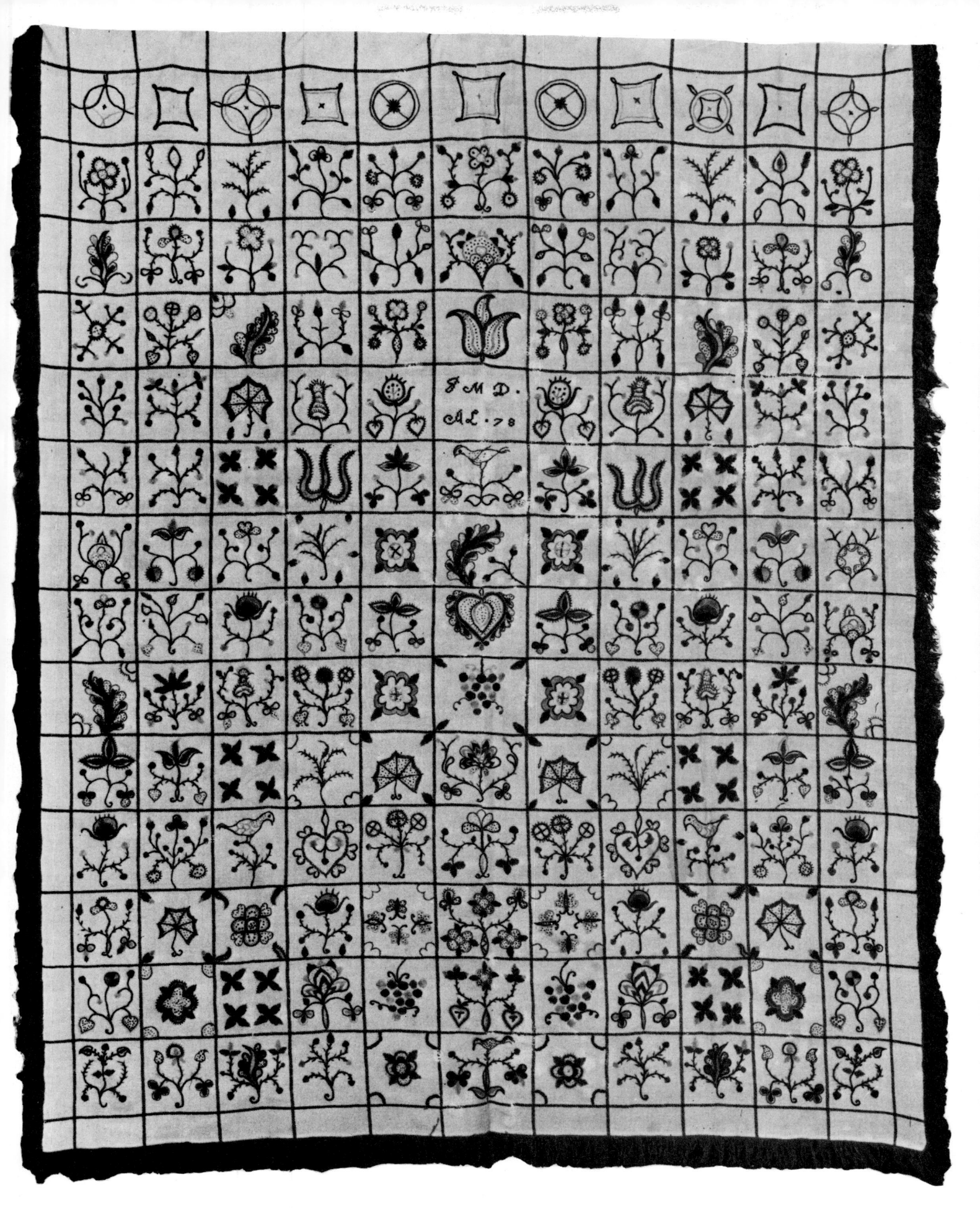

66

The age-old techniques of pottery-making are demonstrated by the Museum potter when he "throws" pots on a kick-wheel. Firing and glazing are completed in a large kiln in Greenfield Village's *Haggerty Power Plant*. The antique pottery collection displayed in the Street of Shops is comprised of several hundred American examples and includes outstanding pieces of redware and sgraffito (scratch-decorated pieces), as well as a large group of decorated gray stoneware. The winsome redware lion *(below)* was fashioned by John Bell (1826–1881) of Waynesboro, Pennsylvania. This Shenandoah Valley piece is covered with a bright yellow slip and its "coleslaw" mane is highlighted with a black glaze.

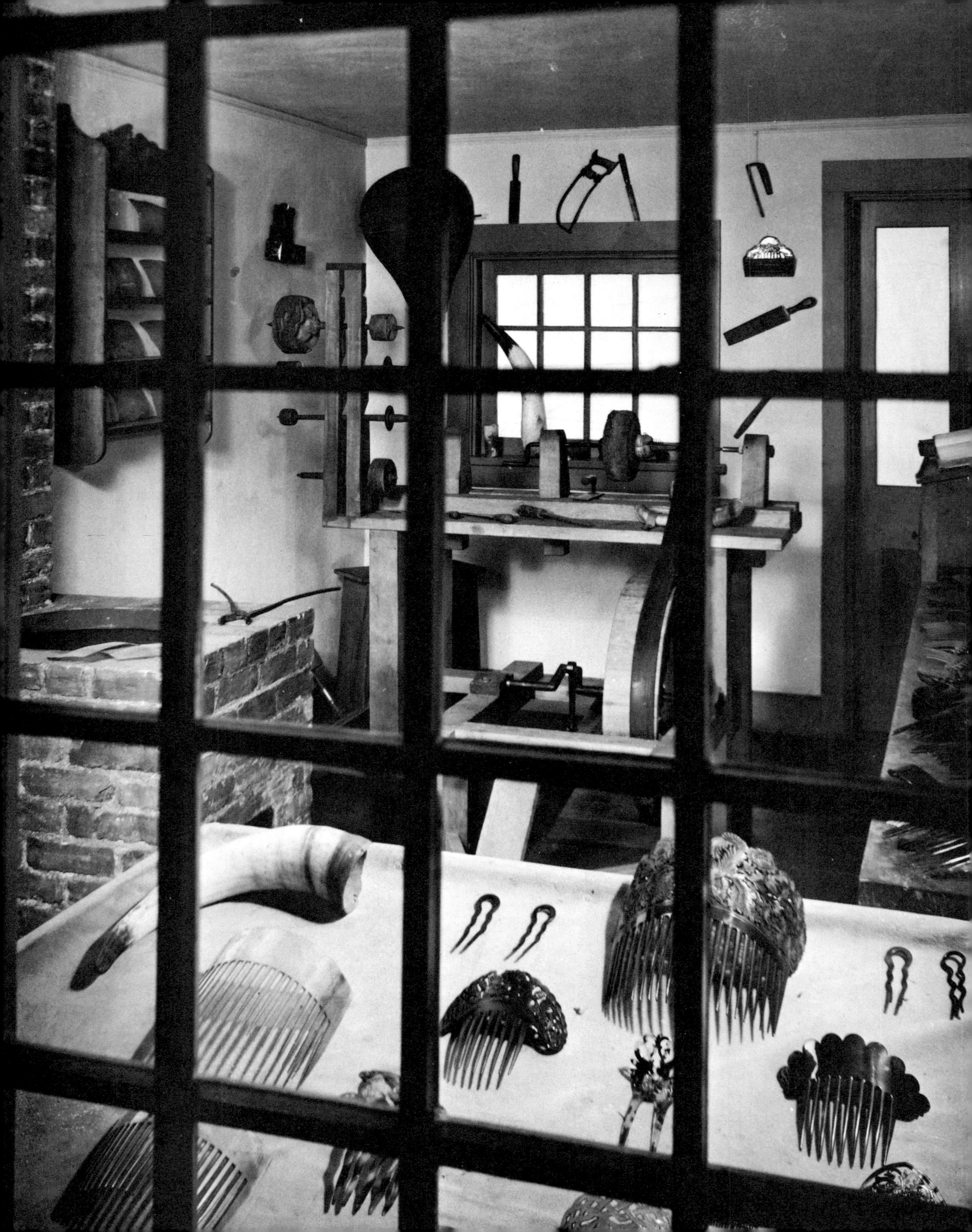

The foot-powered lathe under the rear window in the *Noyes Horn Comb Shop (left)* was employed for sawing and buffing the tortoiseshell used to create the elaborate combs in the window. A variety of small tools was necessary for the final piercing and carving.

Elegantly upholstered barber chairs were comforts provided in the more expensive nineteenth-century barbershops. The plush-upholstered walnut and iron example *(right)* was made in Rochester, New York, circa 1880, by the Archer Manufacturing Company. On the shelves of the *Charles Fowler Barber Shop (below),* there is a gay collection of personalized shaving mugs.

The John F. Brown Gun and Locksmith Shop (right) contains a comprehensive collection of pistols, revolvers, muskets, rifles, shotguns, powderhorns, tomahawks, knives, and swords. Of special interest is a unique set of metal templates used by David Defibaugh, a gunsmith of Bedford County, Pennsylvania, circa 1835, to cut out brass inlay decorations for long rifles *(far right)*. The campaign chest and folding bed *(below)* were both used by General George Washington during the American Revolution. The bed was presented to him by General Peter Gansevoort of Schuylerville, New York. The chest was made in London, England, by William Chapple in 1783 and is fitted with cooking and eating utensils.

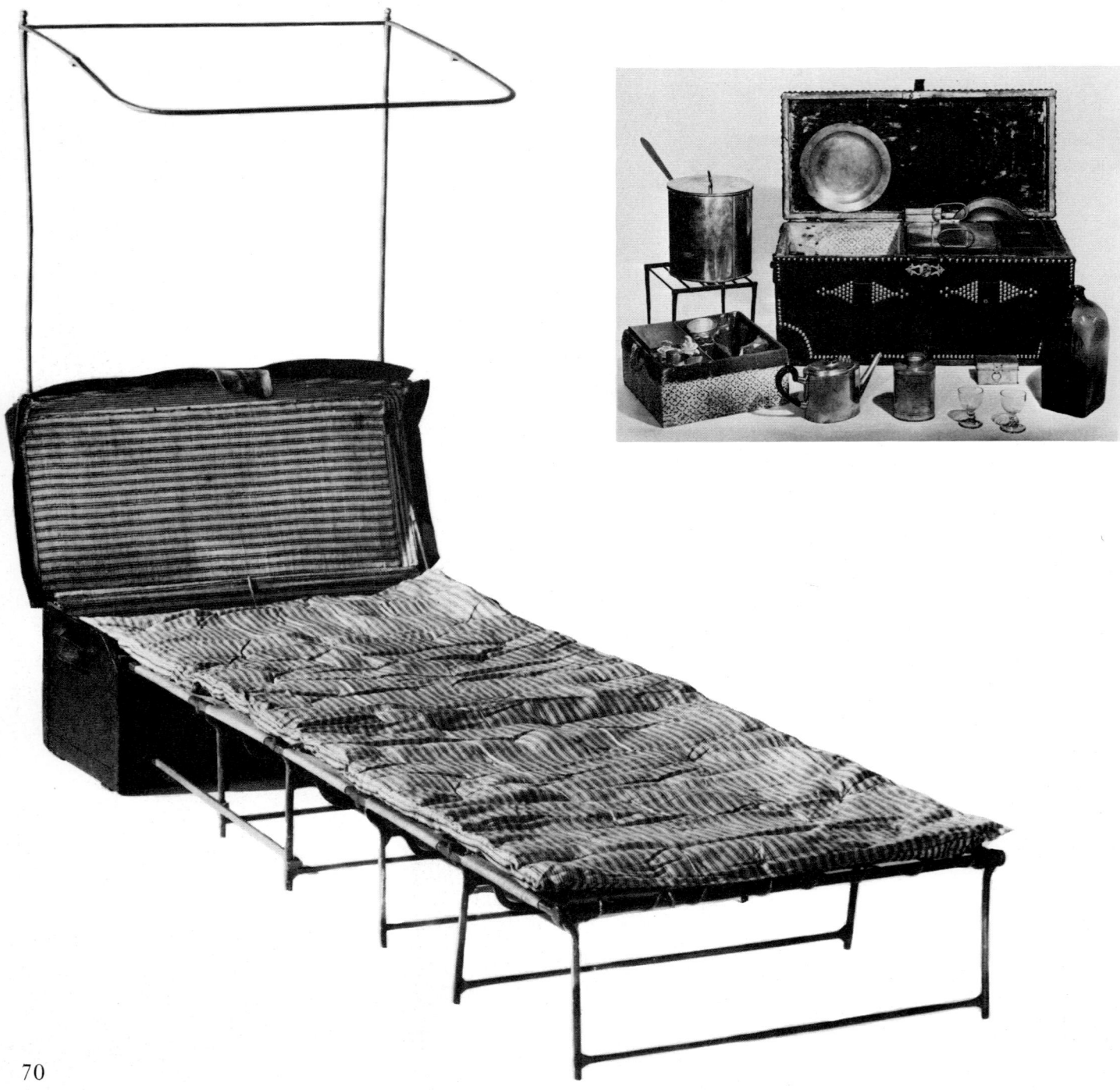

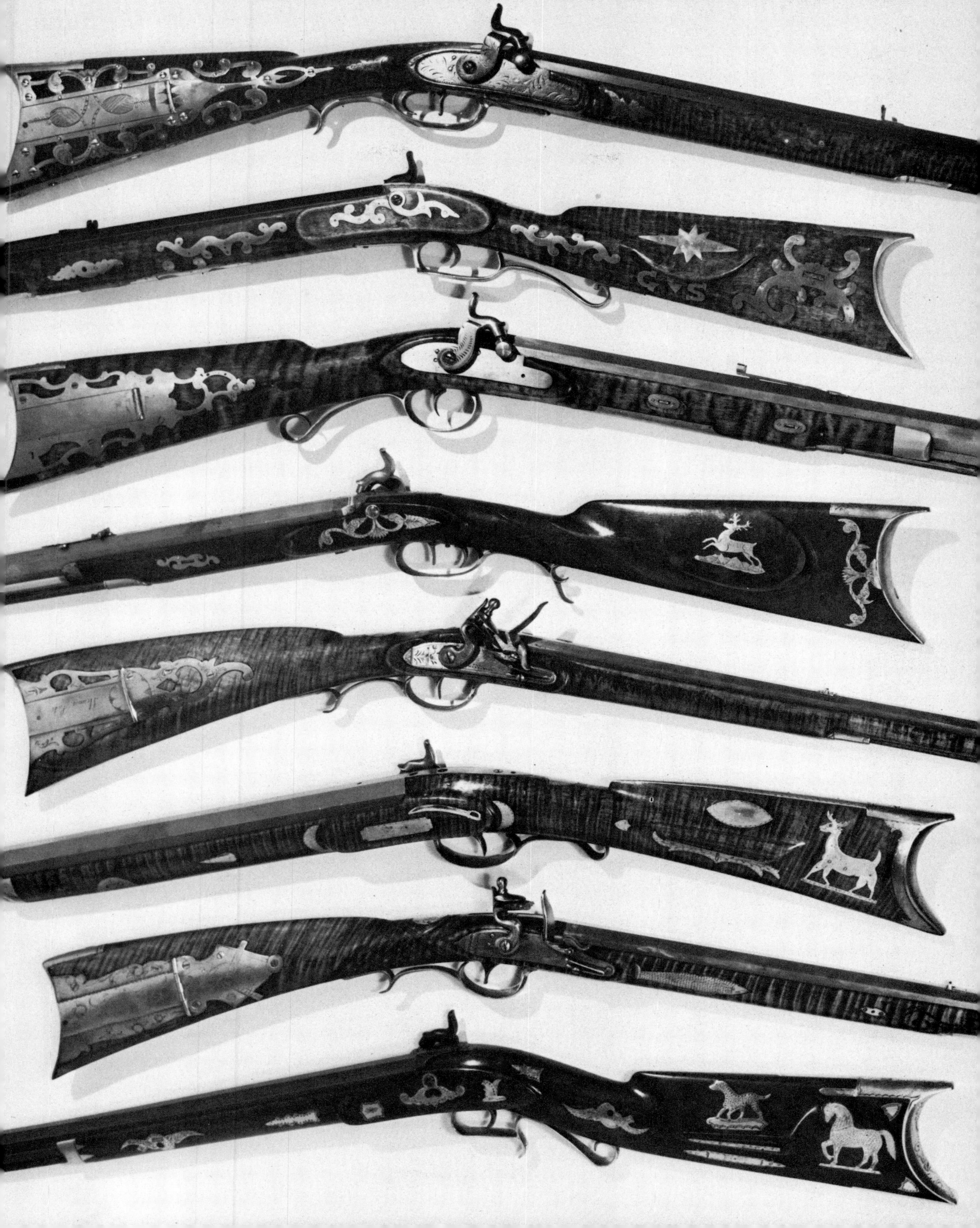
GVS

III. Mechanical Arts Hall

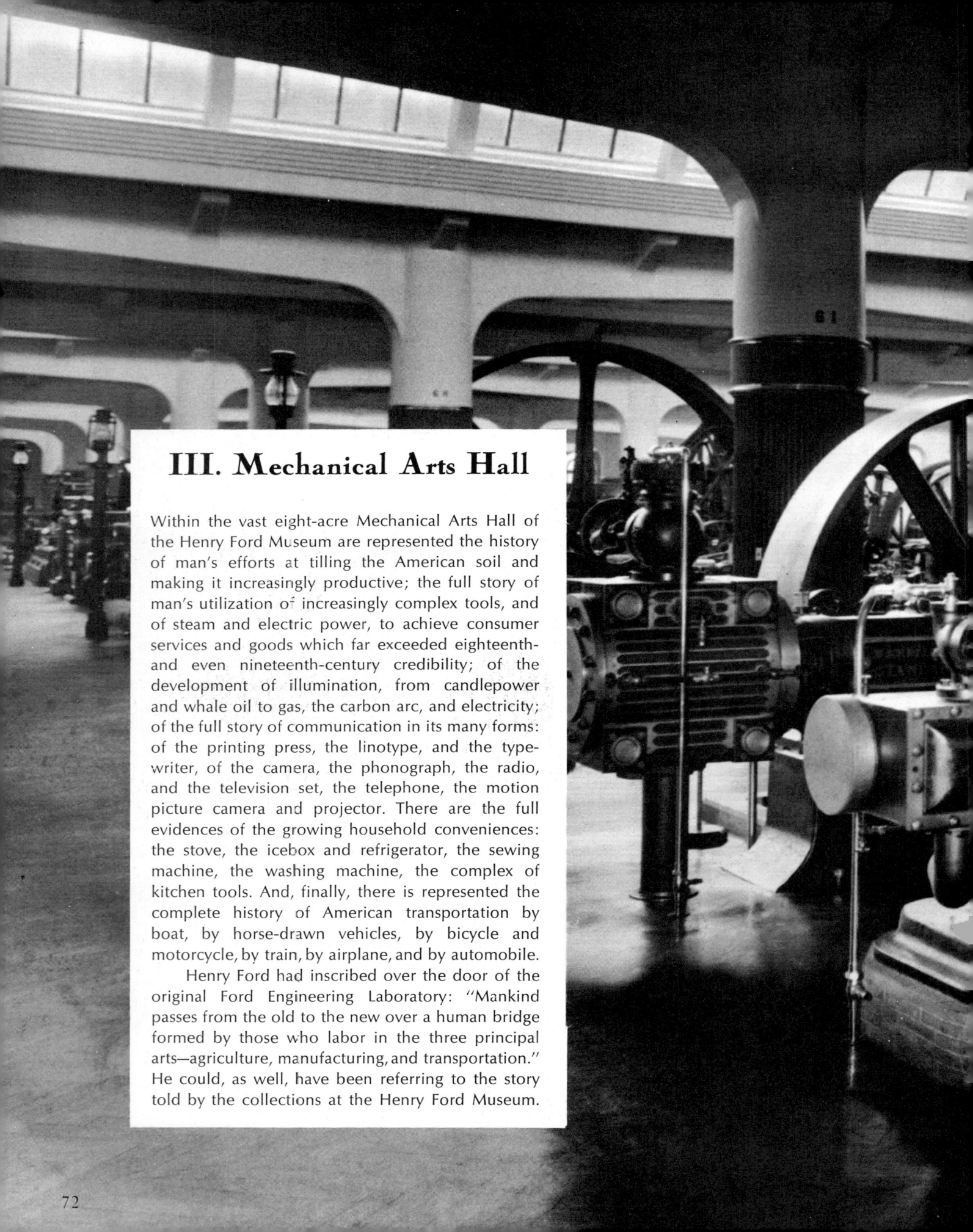

Within the vast eight-acre Mechanical Arts Hall of the Henry Ford Museum are represented the history of man's efforts at tilling the American soil and making it increasingly productive; the full story of man's utilization of increasingly complex tools, and of steam and electric power, to achieve consumer services and goods which far exceeded eighteenth- and even nineteenth-century credibility; of the development of illumination, from candlepower and whale oil to gas, the carbon arc, and electricity; of the full story of communication in its many forms: of the printing press, the linotype, and the typewriter, of the camera, the phonograph, the radio, and the television set, the telephone, the motion picture camera and projector. There are the full evidences of the growing household conveniences: the stove, the icebox and refrigerator, the sewing machine, the washing machine, the complex of kitchen tools. And, finally, there is represented the complete history of American transportation by boat, by horse-drawn vehicles, by bicycle and motorcycle, by train, by airplane, and by automobile.

Henry Ford had inscribed over the door of the original Ford Engineering Laboratory: "Mankind passes from the old to the new over a human bridge formed by those who labor in the three principal arts—agriculture, manufacturing, and transportation." He could, as well, have been referring to the story told by the collections at the Henry Ford Museum.

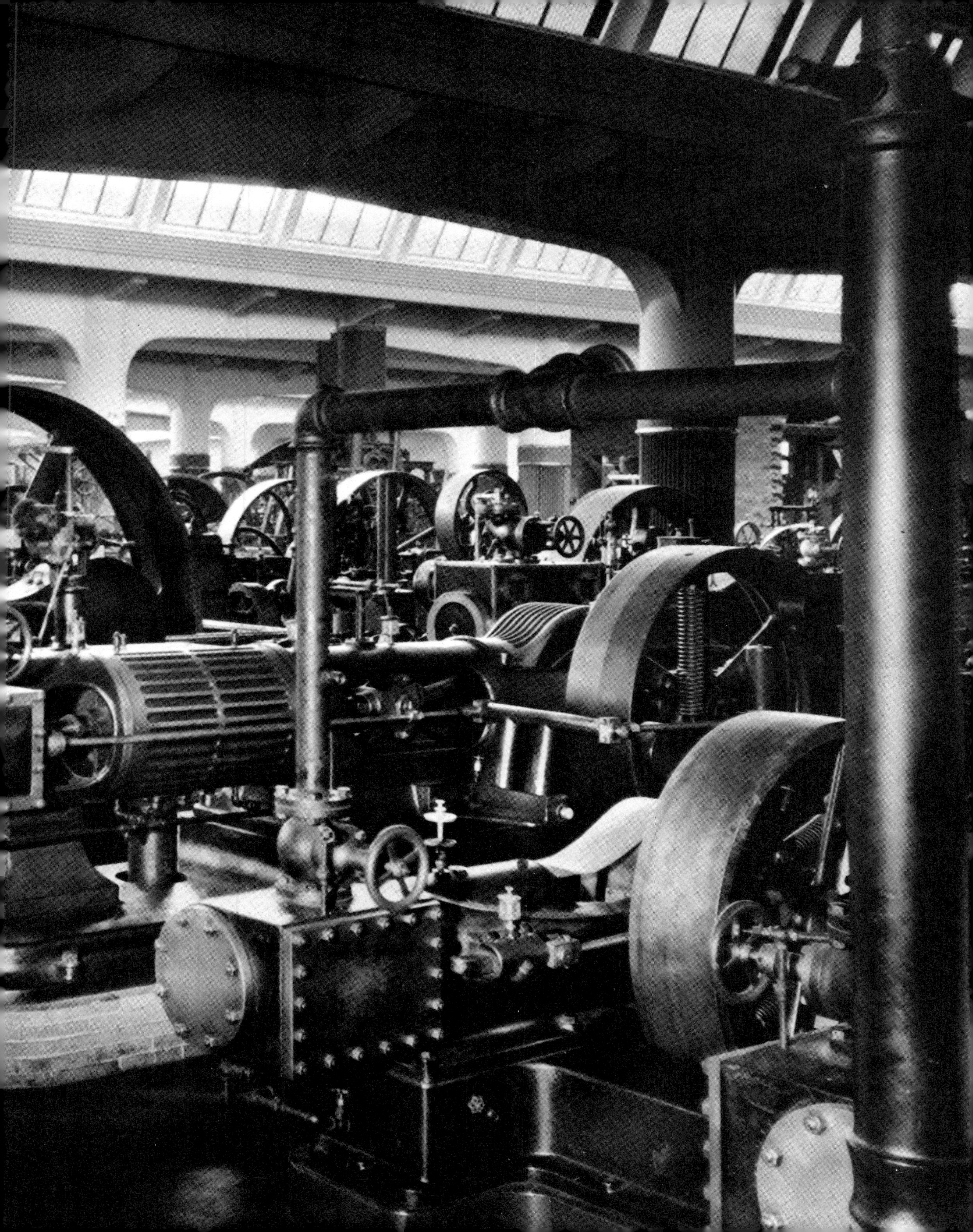

Henry Ford, who was born on a farm, regarded agriculture as one of the principal areas of American economic life which should be preserved in The Edison Institute. The agriculture collection which he began is one of the largest assemblages of farm implements and machines in the world. Collected widely in New England, the mid-Atlantic states, and the Middle West, these objects record some two hundred years of the evolving technology of American agriculture. They are grouped according to the farm activity in which they were used—plowing, seeding, cultivating, harvesting, and threshing grain—and according to the power sources used on farms. Tillage or cultivation involves loosening the soil to prepare and maintain a suitable seedbed for growing plants. The most important instrument of tillage is the plow. It developed from simple wooden handcrafted implements of English and Dutch origin into the factory-produced steel versions of the last one hundred years. Other tillage tools range from the hoe and spade to harrows, rollers, and cultivators.

Left, top: New England "strong plow" with a wooden moldboard sheathed in iron, eighteenth century, Biddeford, Maine.

Near left, top: Early cast iron moldboard plow, circa 1825, I. Tice, Hudson Furnace, Washington County, New York.

Near left, bottom: Chilled iron moldboard plow, late nineteenth century, Oliver Company, South Bend, Indiana.

Left, bottom: Spiked-tooth rotary harrow, circa 1865, Michigan.

Right, top: Grain and fertilizer drill, circa 1895, Superior Company, Springfield, Ohio.

1. Agriculture

Seeding was traditionally done by hand or with the aid of hand tools. During the nineteenth century, many "tinkerers" attempted to develop mechanical substitutes such as the grain drill for this task. These were later adapted to grass seeding and corn planting. Harvesting grain posed the most critical problem for the American farmer. The scarcity of labor and the short harvesting season determined how large a crop he could plant. Using the common grain harvesting tool of the eighteenth century—the sickle—one man could reap from one-half to three-quarters of an acre per day. The grain cradle increased this performance to about two acres. An extra man was required to bind the cut grain into sheaves and to stack them in shocks. The mechanical reaper, first developed in the 1830s by Cyrus H. McCormick and Obed Hussey, produced profound changes in this situation. Even these earliest reapers averaged from ten to twelve acres per day, with one man driving and one raking the cut grain. The later self-raking reaper of the 1860s eliminated one of these men, and the automatic binder, developed during the 1870s, ended the need for the four or more men binding after each machine.

Above: Grain cradle, mid-nineteenth century.

Right, top: Replica of Cyrus H. McCormick's 1834 patent reaper.

Below: Self-raking reaper, circa 1872, D. M. Osborn and Company, Auburn, New York.

Cereal grasses have always been among the most important American crops. Between harvesting and marketing, the crops must be threshed, separated, and cleaned. Two methods of threshing were used in early America—animal treading, in which the weight of the horses' hooves broke open the husk, and flailing, where frequent blows from a heavy wooden tool achieved the same result. The grain was separated by raking the stalks of the plant aside and shoveling the seed, mixed with the chaff and dirt, into a pile. This mixture was then poured from a winnowing basket or "fan," allowing the wind to carry away the lighter impurities while the heavier grain fell to the ground. Fanning mills, introduced early in the nineteenth century, improved this process by using an artificial blast of air and sifting screens of varying sizes. After the development of the mechanical threshing machine later in the nineteenth century, these three operations were combined.

Right, bottom: Fanning mill, M. Elliot's patent, 1831, Massachusetts.

Below: Threshing machine, circa 1850, Watertown Agricultural Works, Watertown, New York.

Above: Steam threshing scene from an 1884 catalogue of J. I. Case Company, Racine, Wisconsin.

Below: Flail and winnowing basket, mid-nineteenth century.

The mechanization of American agriculture—particularly of threshing—pointed up the need for new sources of power to replace the traditional horse and ox. During the nineteenth century, steam was universally thought to be the answer. In 1849, small portable steam engines, built specifically to power threshing machines, became available. In order to replace the horse completely, a "steam plow," or self-propelled steam traction engine, was necessary. It was not until the 1870s that the first reliable traction engines came into use. Because of their size, extreme weight, and cost, these engines were practicable only on larger farms, particularly in the West. It was the lightweight gasoline tractor of the twentieth century which finally supplied the long-sought power needs of the average American farmer.

Above: Portable steam engine, circa 1878, Fishkill Landing Machine Company, Fishkill, New York.

Right: Collection of ponderous traction and portable steam engines on exhibit in the Henry Ford Museum.

Below: Henry Ford demonstrating his earliest tractor, an experimental model of 1907–1908.

Today, in the era of liberated women, many of whom work outside the home, housework is fitted into and around other schedules. Before the days of packaged foods, wrinkle-free fabrics, and automatic appliances, housework was done on a rigorously followed schedule: Monday, washing; Tuesday, ironing; Wednesday, sewing; Thursday, shopping; Friday, cleaning; and Saturday, baking.

The domestic arts collections in the Henry Ford Museum illustrate the changes in American homemaking techniques from the seventeenth through the early twentieth century. These collections demonstrate the progress in homemaking from hearth cookery and handmade implements to the present age of mechanization.

During the middle and late nineteenth century, improved technology produced appliances such as the 1867 Singer Sewing Machine *(left, center)*, made in New York, and the Jewel Coal-Saving Range *(far left, top)* of the 1880s to lighten the homemaker's job. And rather than use a washtub for the laundry, she could now use one of the many washing machines, such as the Boss Washing Machine *(below)*, patented in 1888.

Although she probably still used handmade wooden bowls *(left, bottom)*, she now had her choice of factory-made kitchen implements.

Hand-decorated mass-produced tin kitchens *(right)* were used for storing flour, coffee, and spices safely. Tin pastry boards with a built-in shelf for storing the accompanying rolling pin were also available.

2. Domestic Arts

The story of civilization has recorded many attempts to develop improved methods of artificial illumination. Until man mastered artificial lighting, his activities were confined to the daylight hours.

In 1879 Thomas Edison made electric light a practicality. Henry Ford greatly admired Edison's contribution and honored him by forming a lighting collection to illustrate the development of lighting in the United States from the period of household improvisation to that of industrialization.

During the period of America's first settlement, candles, rushlights, and grease lamps were the prime sources of artificial light. Aside from those few articles which were imported, each household was responsible for creating its own lighting implements. Wrought iron rush holders from the seventeenth century *(near right and bottom left)* were commonly brought to America from England and the Continent.

When craft shops developed, the manufacture of lighting devices moved from the home to professional workers in iron, tin, and pottery. Blacksmiths, like Peter Derr, Berks County, Pennsylvania, made lamps. Derr's brass, copper, and iron betty *(above center)* is dated 1848. Betty lamps were also mounted on stands and were adjustable *(center)* like this Ohio example.

American potters like S. Routson from Ohio, working in the 1840s, contributed to the development of lighting devices by making pottery grease lamps *(right, center)*.

Among lighting devices of European origin are the water refractors *(right)* used by lacemakers, cobblers, and watchmakers to intensify candlelight. These ingenious devices were the forerunners of the later bull's-eye lamps. A woodcut *(right, top)* from John White's *Art Treasury*, 1688, illustrates how these devices were used.

3. Lighting

81

82

A NEW AND SUPERIOR LAMP, FOR BURNING LARD.

The Patent Adjustable Lard Lamp.

This Lamp makes a very economical light, cheaper than Oil or Fluid, is easily adjusted and kept in burning order and will afford more light than any other now in use for the same consumption of burning material. One half pound of Lard will last Sixteen Hours, and give throughout that time a very brilliant light, with no other care than now and then turning the wrench so as force the Lard up against the wick.

☞ The proprietors of this Lamp received a Diploma at the last State Fair, and the Lamp itself has given universal satisfaction whenever used.

Directions for Using the Lamp.

Take a piece of coarse open Cotton Flannel or Drilling the width of the iron slide, put it in double, then unscrew the packing and with a knife fill the cylinder with cold Lard, then adjust the packing on the spiral screw and with the thumb wrench, screw the packing down until the lard comes up to the wick. When a new wick is put in the lamp apply a little lard on the top of the wick before lighting, that the blaze may have some lard to feed upon until the heat melts the lard in the tube.

In cold weather, before extinguishing the light, press the lard up to the wick, then it will be ready for use when wanting.

Manufactured and for sale Wholesale and Retail by the subscribers, sole Proprietors for the N. E. States.

TILTON & SLEEPER,
Fremont, N. H.

Lard and lard oil lamps were indigenous to the United States. During the second quarter of the nineteenth century inventors, in their search for a substitute for costly whale oil, turned to lard as a lamp fuel.

The hanging tin and brass lard oil solar lamp *(upper left)* was manufactured by Cornelius & Co., Philadelphia, and is based upon Robert Cornelius's patent of April 18, 1843. The pewter chandelier *(lower left),* made by William S. Lawrence of Meriden, Connecticut, has three decorated pewter fish fonts mounted around his patented 1834 lard burner. The tin lamp *(above left)* was patented by Zuriel Swope on March 13, 1860, in Lancaster, Pennsylvania. Tilton & Sleeper, Freemont, New Hampshire, manufactured the tin lamp *(above right)* using the I. Smith and J. Stonesifer patent granted August 8, 1854, in Boonsboro, Maryland.

Although lard lamps came into common use, whale oil was not totally displaced. Among the very rare patented whale oil lighting devices is the railroad conductor's lantern *(right),* patented by Philos Blake on January 13, 1852, in New Haven, Connecticut, and manufactured by D. D. Miller in New York.

American artifacts comprise the bulk of the Henry Ford Museum's lighting collection *(below)*, but lighting devices from ancient civilizations and foreign countries are also represented.

Many fine examples of political parade torches are included. The gilded sheet copper, eagle-shaped torch *(left)* was used for campaigns during the 1860s.

An outstanding example of the Boston and Sandwich Glass Company's production is an overlay glass lamp fitted with a double kerosene burner *(right)*. This lamp dates from about 1875, and is one of the tallest of its kind.

The gilded wood and gesso electric chandelier *(opposite)* was designed for and used in "Fair Lane," Henry Ford's Dearborn home, which he and Mrs. Ford first occupied in 1915.

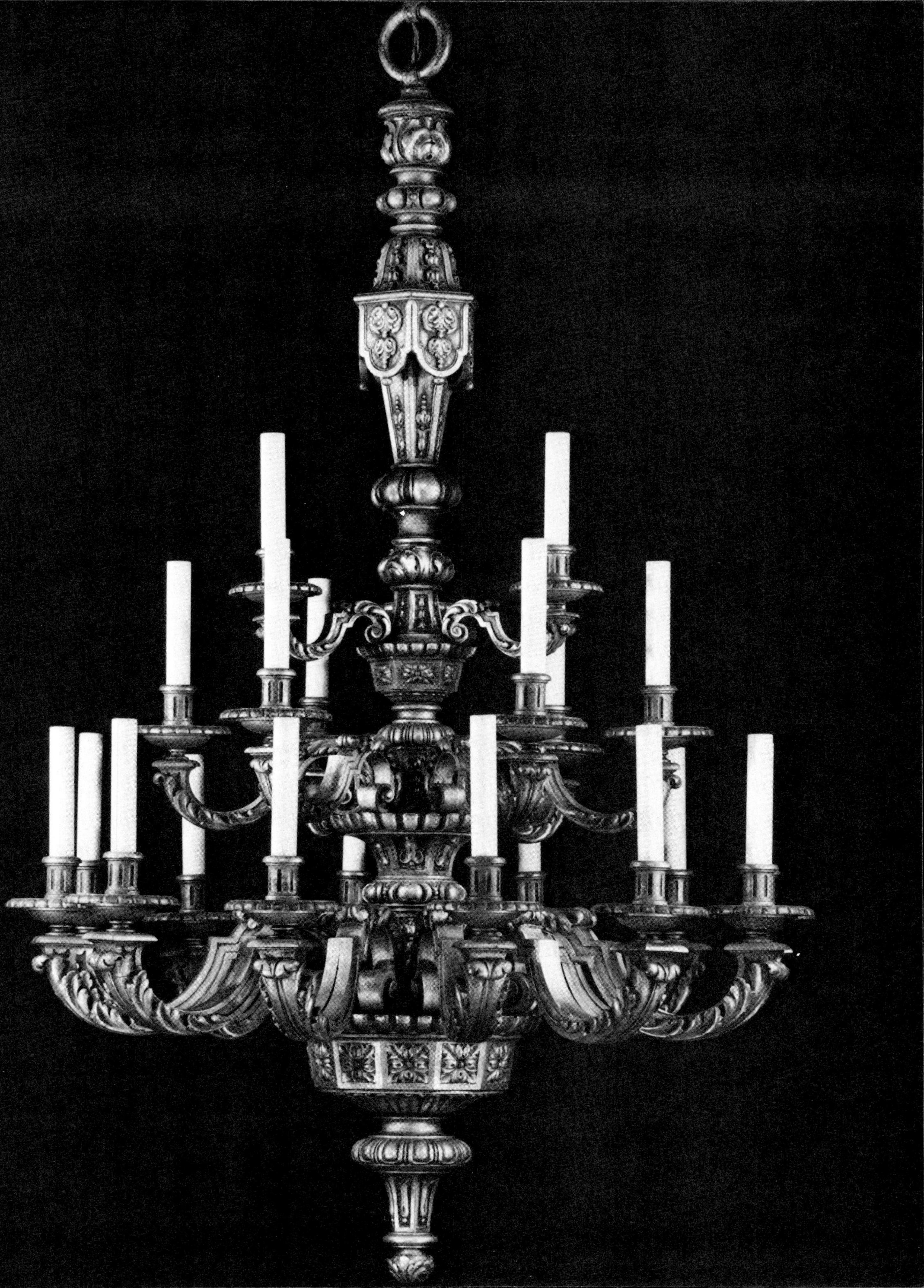

The Columbian Steam Engine.

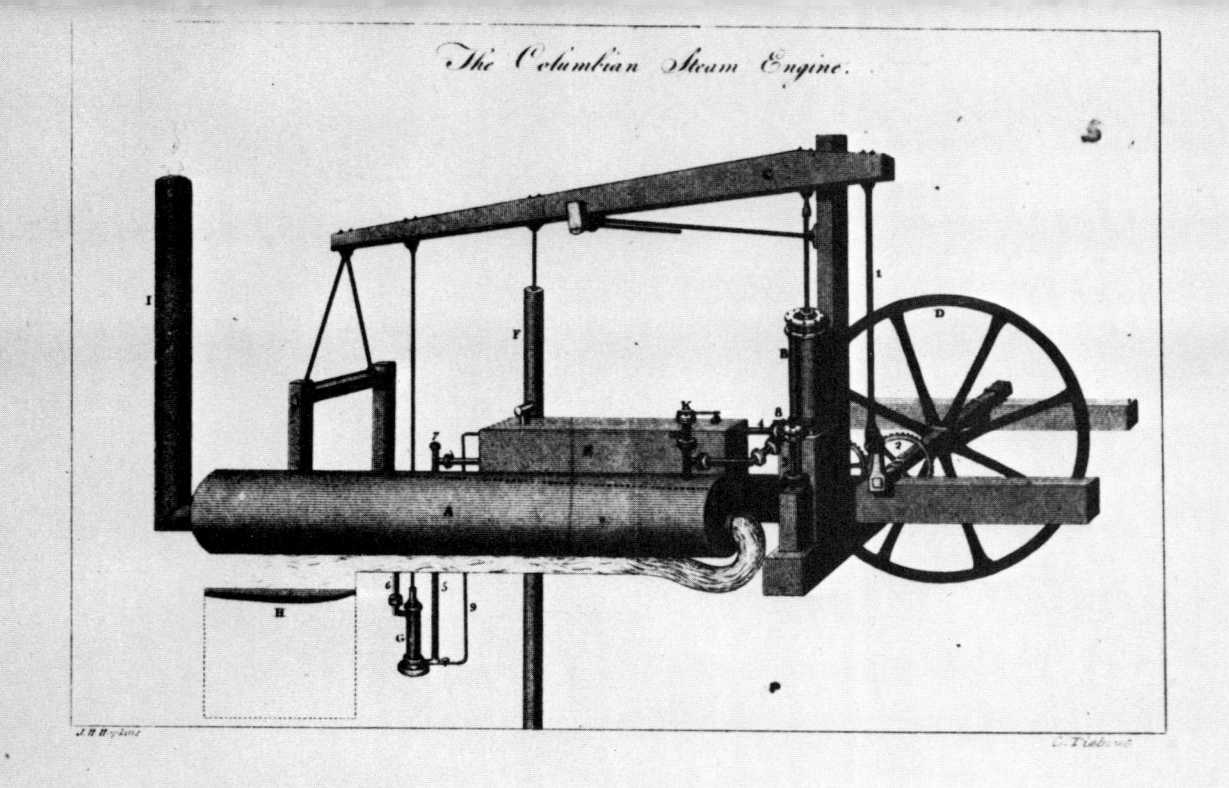

LICENSE.

KNOW all Men by these presents, That I, Oliver Evans, Steam-Engineer, of the city of Philadelphia, have received of *The Marrietta Steam Mill Co.* of *the state of Ohio* county, state of *Ohio* the sum of *Four Hundred & eighty Dollars* in full payment for a Steam-Engine, and for License hereby granted to the said *Marrietta Steam Mill Co. their* heirs, executors, administrators and assigns, to use one of my patented Steam-Engines, constructed on the principle of retaining the steam in strong boilers, in order to increase the heat, and thereby increase the elastic power of the steam until they obtain the power of *Twenty* horses to be exerted by *their* engine: The power of a horse to be rated at 150 pounds raised perpendicularly 220 feet per minute,—or the piston of the engine to describe 7920 cubic inches of space per minute, (for each horse power) carrying an average load of 50 pounds to each superficial square inch of the area of its end; according to the rules laid down for ascertaining the power of my steam-engine, in my book entitled "The Abortion of the Young Steam-Engineer's Guide," and to apply and use the same *in Marrietta State of Ohio to the grinding of grain or to any other purposes whatever*

for and during my present or any future patent term. Witness my hand and seal this *Tenth* day of *November 1812*

Witness present

Lemuel Johnson
James McIntosh
Stackhouse & Rogers

Oliver Evans
Geo. Evans patent ag
for Oliver Evans

4. Power

The Industrial Revolution, which created modern society and civilization, began with the development of the steam engine. One of the world's largest and most complete collections of steam engines, showing the development of this prime mover from its beginnings at the hand of Thomas Newcomen (1663–1729) in the eighteenth century to modern times, is at the Henry Ford Museum. The oldest complete atmospheric steam engine in the collection, and perhaps in the world *(right)*, came from the Chambers Colliery near Ashton-under-Lyne in Lancashire, England, where it was used to pump water from a mine beginning about 1760.

The second major development of the steam engine was undertaken by James Watt (1736–1819) between the years 1765 and 1788. He doubled engine efficiency by adding a separate condenser and by using the steam to push the piston from either side. He also added a governor which helped to maintain a steady speed, and developed innovations which changed the movement of the atmospheric engine from a to-and-fro motion to a rotary motion. These alterations made the engine more adaptable to factory work. An exact duplicate of Watt's famous Sun-and-Planet engine of 1788 *(below)* incorporates all these improvements. There are other original Watt-type engines on display.

Watt believed that only low pressure should be used in a steam engine; however, high pressure was to be the direction of future development. Oliver Evans (1755–1819) was one of the first Americans to build high-pressure engines. He issued a license *(left)* on November 10, 1812, to the "Mariatta Steam Mill Company" at Marietta, Ohio, for the operation of a twenty-horsepower reciprocating beam engine which he sold to the firm for "grinding of grain or to any other purposes whatever. . . ."

Despite the fact that the Watt engines were more efficient than the earlier atmospheric engines, the latter continued to be built for several decades after Watt and his business partner, Matthew Boulton, began selling theirs in 1774. The late atmospheric engine and engine house *(below)* were probably built around 1800 and were used for pumping water at Windmill End Station, Netherton, Dudley, Worcestershire, England, until 1928. It is interesting to note that the engine has both a crank and a separate condenser. The small English engine *(left, top),* from the Howe Dye Works in England, was used from the time of its construction in 1830 until a century later. The well-known nineteenth-century American engine *(left, middle)* built by C. H. Brown at Fitchburg, Massachusetts, in 1881, was popular because of its high efficiency and reliability.

By the end of the nineteenth century, the steam engine, at least in many smaller installations, was supplanted by a newcomer—the internal combustion engine *(right).* The taller engine, with a capacity of approximately two horsepower, was made about 1875 by the English firm of Crossley Brothers under the 1867 English patents of Nicholas Otto and Eugene Langen. Although this early Otto and Langen engine was quite noisy and at times vibrated considerably, it was widely used until replaced by their four-stroke engine of 1878. The shorter engine with a capacity of about one-half horsepower, built about a decade later by the English firm of J. E. H. Andrew, Stockport, England, under the 1872 and 1875 patents of A. deBisschop, was dependable and simple to operate.

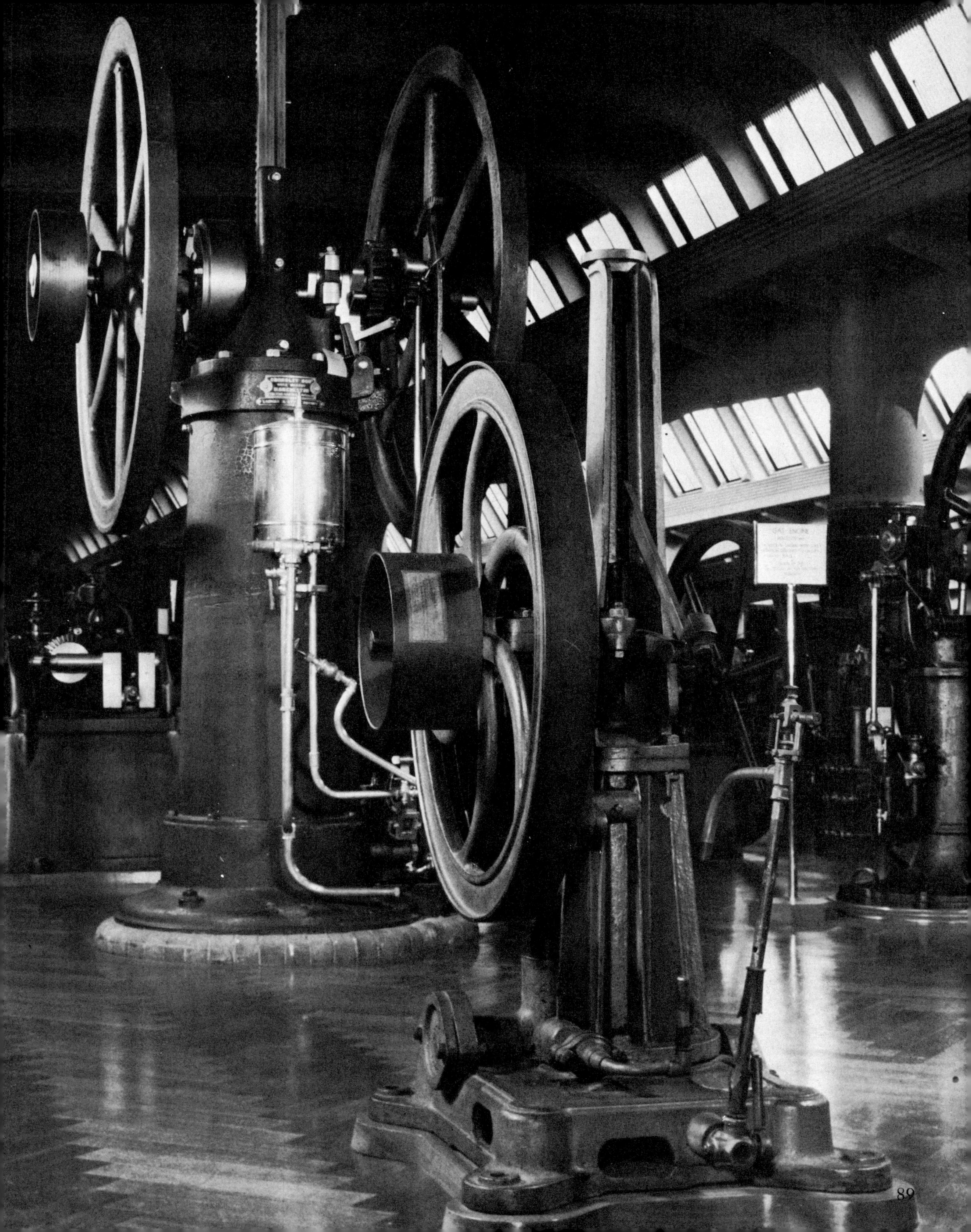

5. Machinery

Though ancient Greece has long been considered the cradle of the fine arts, that civilization also made many contributions to the field of practical technology. One of its most important developments was the lathe. The wooden lathe of antiquity did not begin to change in design until the end of the eighteenth century, when iron and steel were used for its construction. The pole lathe *(above)*, constructed by a nineteenth-century American woodworker, is similar in many ways to its Greek prototype.

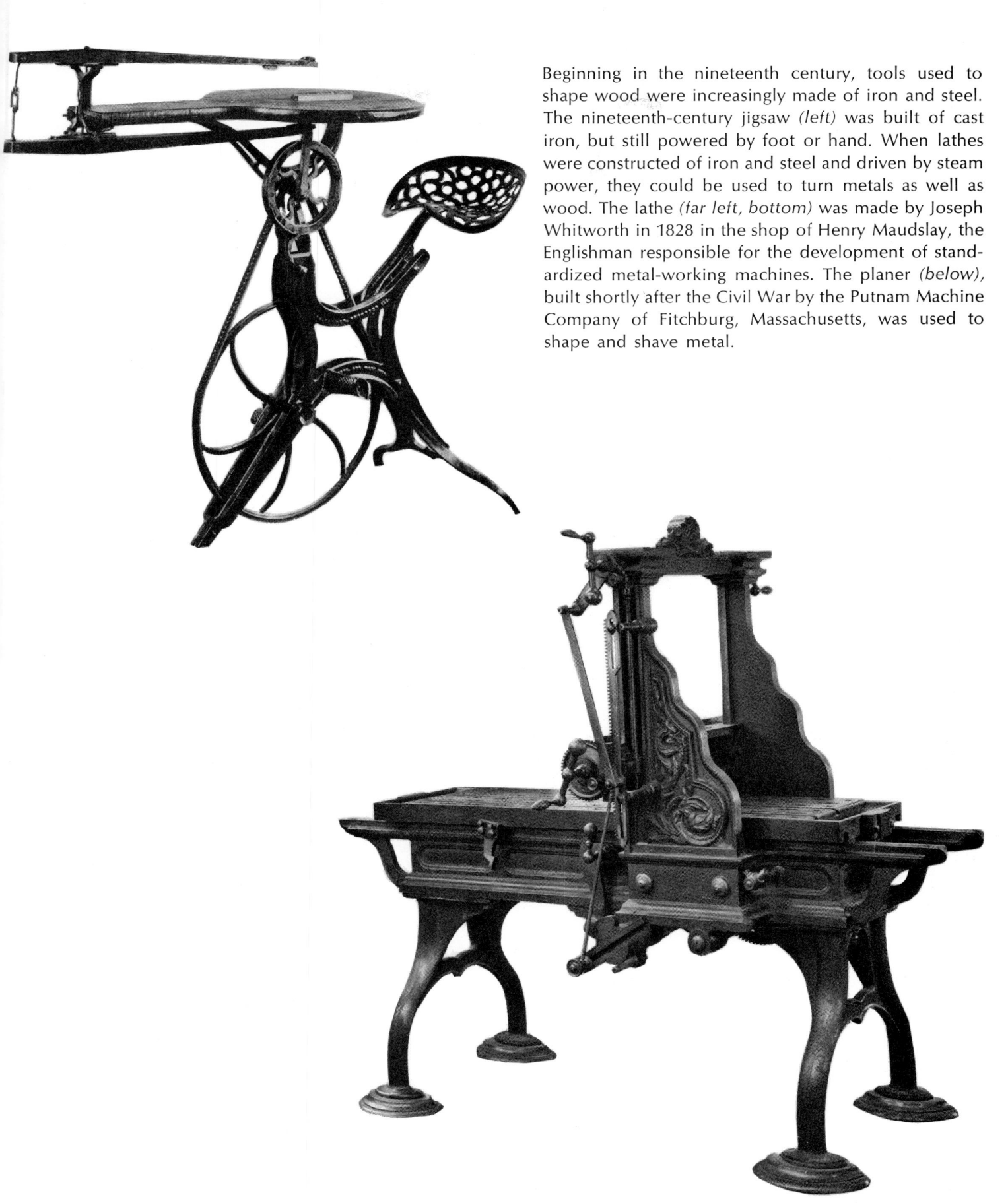

Beginning in the nineteenth century, tools used to shape wood were increasingly made of iron and steel. The nineteenth-century jigsaw *(left)* was built of cast iron, but still powered by foot or hand. When lathes were constructed of iron and steel and driven by steam power, they could be used to turn metals as well as wood. The lathe *(far left, bottom)* was made by Joseph Whitworth in 1828 in the shop of Henry Maudslay, the Englishman responsible for the development of standardized metal-working machines. The planer *(below)*, built shortly after the Civil War by the Putnam Machine Company of Fitchburg, Massachusetts, was used to shape and shave metal.

Great advances in communications—photography, telegraphy, printing—and in the field of applied electricity were realized in the nineteenth century. One of the earliest practical methods of photography was developed by the Frenchman, Louis J. M. Daguerre, in 1839. His process, which spread rapidly throughout the world, was brought to America by inventor Samuel F. B. Morse. The wooden camera and tripod *(left),* constructed about 1845, is one of the earliest complete Daguerrean outfits known. The 1889 Edison camera marked the transition from still photography to motion pictures. The model *(below)* was probably made in 1896 for the Mutoscope patent trials, where it was used to prove Edison's prior involvement with the practical development of the motion picture.

6. Communications

The process of printing was improved in a number of ways during the nineteenth century. From the days of Gutenberg in the mid-1400s, most printing presses had been constructed of wood and utilized a large screw to apply pressure to the type and paper. In 1813, Edward Bevan, an Englishman, introduced the Columbian press. It was an all-iron machine in which the speed of printing was increased by replacing the screw with a variation of a toggle joint. The Columbian press was further improved in 1821 by Samuel Rust, inventor of the Washington press *(left, below)*. This example, made by the famous R. Hoe Company of New York City, contributed much to American history. Sometime in the late 1840s it was purchased by "Judge" J. Judson Ames of Baton Rouge, Louisiana, who printed the newspaper that helped elect Zachary Taylor to the presidency in 1848. Like so many Americans in 1849, Ames went to California in search of gold. There he sold the press to Major E. Sherman, who, during the early years of the Civil War, advocated the Union cause so strongly in his journal that he was forced to protect his press with an armed guard. Sherman moved to Aurora, Nevada, where he founded the *Esmeralda Star* in 1862. It was at that time that the young Mark Twain used this press.

The invention of the typewriter made a large contribution toward the economic independence of women in the nineteenth century. The 1874 model *(right, below)*, manufactured by the Remington Arms Company under the Sholes-Glidden patent of 1868, is one of the earliest mass-produced, commercially-practical typewriters.

Advances in printing occurred through the mechanization of the type-composing process. The keyboard-composing machine *(above),* an early form of linotype machine, was devised in 1891 by H. Lee and E. LeBrun. It made a matrix in which the text for an entire page could be cast.

The small telegraph set *(left, bottom),* manufactured by Hugo Gernsback, one of the foremost pioneers in the development of the commercial wireless, was marketed in the form of a "do-it-yourself" kit in 1906. It was the first production wireless telegraph in the world to be advertised for sale. Many of the electrical experimenters of the day obtained their initial experience with what was later to be termed "radio" from a gadget like this.

The phonograph helped inaugurate the American home entertainment industry. One of the more elegant versions *(right)* was made about 1910 following the Edison patents of February 1878. It is interesting to note that Edison, almost from the beginning, attempted to enhance his motion picture system by synchronizing it with recorded sound.

Until the twentieth century, the application of electricity to the needs of mankind was a very slow process. In the last quarter of the eighteenth century, electrostatic machines *(above)*, similar to this one made by I. M. Wightman in Boston, Massachusetts, were fashioned. The device replaced the primitive method of making electric sparks by rubbing glass and animal fur together. More than a century elapsed before generators for electric lighting were developed.

Thomas Alva Edison, who perfected a direct current system between 1878 and 1882, was the first to devise a practical, commercial method of illuminating the home with incandescent light from a central power station. The steamship *Columbia,* voyaging from New York around Cape Horn to Portland, Oregon, was equipped with one of Edison's earliest commercial incandescent lamp installations powered by the Edison bipolar generator *(right),* which was dubbed the "Long-legged Mary Ann." The more familiar 1882 Edison generator *(far left, bottom),* designed and constructed at the Edison Machine Works at Schenectady, New York, soon replaced the 1880 "Mary Ann."

Because of economic considerations, the Edison direct current system was limited in its transmission of power to distances of a mile or less. During the early 1890s, the alternating current systems of Westinghouse and General Electric superseded it. The Westinghouse meter *(near left, bottom),* devised by Shallenberger in 1888, measured this relatively new form of current. The General Electric rotary converter *(below),* which appeared in the early 1890s, was a combination AC motor–DC generator device that transformed alternating current to direct current. It gave the alternating system all the advantages of direct current with little power loss during transmission.

The nineteenth and twentieth centuries saw a steady increase in the exploitation of electricity for the field of communications—the telegraph of the 1830s, the telephone of the 1870s, radio of the 1890s, and television of the 1920s. In the Museum installation *(bottom)* are two of the more important advances in wire communications—Edison's quadruplex telegraph of 1874, which enabled four messages to be sent simultaneously over the same wire, and the step-by-step system telephone switchboard, introduced on a large scale about 1920. The wall magneto telephone *(right)*, although used until relatively recently, dates from the mid-1830s.

Radio broadcasts to the general public began around 1920. The early RCA Radiola *(below)*, manufactured about 1924, was one of the more popular receivers. Headphones were necessary, since the set was not powerful enough to drive a loudspeaker.

Attempts made during the nineteenth century to transmit pictures by telegraph were not especially successful. Once radio broadcasting became popular, inventors attempted to devise ways to transmit pictures by wireless or, as we know it, television. C. Francis Jenkins, a motion picture apparatus inventor of Washington, D.C., developed in 1923 the optical scanner *(far right)*. This device was used to create signals that could be converted to electrical impulses which then could be transmitted by wireless.

99

100

7. Transportation

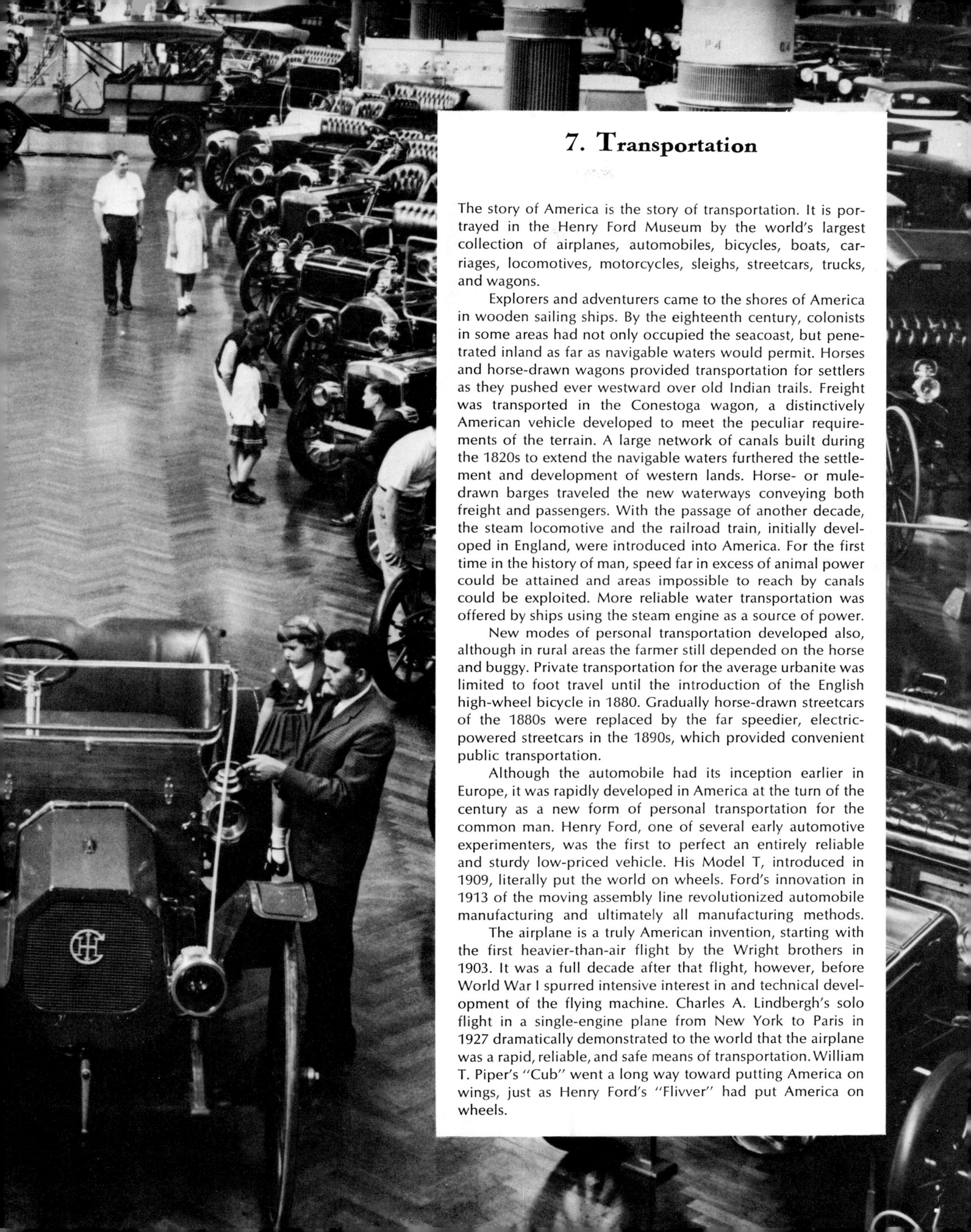

The story of America is the story of transportation. It is portrayed in the Henry Ford Museum by the world's largest collection of airplanes, automobiles, bicycles, boats, carriages, locomotives, motorcycles, sleighs, streetcars, trucks, and wagons.

Explorers and adventurers came to the shores of America in wooden sailing ships. By the eighteenth century, colonists in some areas had not only occupied the seacoast, but penetrated inland as far as navigable waters would permit. Horses and horse-drawn wagons provided transportation for settlers as they pushed ever westward over old Indian trails. Freight was transported in the Conestoga wagon, a distinctively American vehicle developed to meet the peculiar requirements of the terrain. A large network of canals built during the 1820s to extend the navigable waters furthered the settlement and development of western lands. Horse- or mule-drawn barges traveled the new waterways conveying both freight and passengers. With the passage of another decade, the steam locomotive and the railroad train, initially developed in England, were introduced into America. For the first time in the history of man, speed far in excess of animal power could be attained and areas impossible to reach by canals could be exploited. More reliable water transportation was offered by ships using the steam engine as a source of power.

New modes of personal transportation developed also, although in rural areas the farmer still depended on the horse and buggy. Private transportation for the average urbanite was limited to foot travel until the introduction of the English high-wheel bicycle in 1880. Gradually horse-drawn streetcars of the 1880s were replaced by the far speedier, electric-powered streetcars in the 1890s, which provided convenient public transportation.

Although the automobile had its inception earlier in Europe, it was rapidly developed in America at the turn of the century as a new form of personal transportation for the common man. Henry Ford, one of several early automotive experimenters, was the first to perfect an entirely reliable and sturdy low-priced vehicle. His Model T, introduced in 1909, literally put the world on wheels. Ford's innovation in 1913 of the moving assembly line revolutionized automobile manufacturing and ultimately all manufacturing methods.

The airplane is a truly American invention, starting with the first heavier-than-air flight by the Wright brothers in 1903. It was a full decade after that flight, however, before World War I spurred intensive interest in and technical development of the flying machine. Charles A. Lindbergh's solo flight in a single-engine plane from New York to Paris in 1927 dramatically demonstrated to the world that the airplane was a rapid, reliable, and safe means of transportation. William T. Piper's "Cub" went a long way toward putting America on wings, just as Henry Ford's "Flivver" had put America on wheels.

The Association of Licensed Automobile Manufacturers purchased from George Selden his 1895 patent for a "forecarriage." In 1903 the Association, which operated as a monopoly to control the construction of automobiles, sued Henry Ford for infringement of the Selden patent. This car, built by Selden in 1907, proved to the court that his patent was workable. However, the patent was declared valid only for two-cycle engines and the court held that Henry Ford's four-cycle engine did not constitute an infringement. The suit was dismissed and Mr. Ford thus became known as the "trust buster." The dismissal ultimately freed the whole automobile industry from the burden of paying royalties to the ALAM.

The first production Ford, this 1903 Model A Runabout, firmly established the permanence of the Ford Motor Company.

In 1902, Henry Ford designed and built this pioneer racer, dubbed "999," after a fast New York Central locomotive. Driven by Barney Oldfield, "999" became world-famous as a consistent race winner and record breaker. In 1904, Henry Ford personally drove "999" on the ice of Lake St. Clair to set a one-mile record at 91.4 miles per hour. The "999" engine has an impressive 1157-cubic-inch displacement.

Cadillac Runabout, 1903
One-cylinder, chain-driven automobile produced by Henry Leland.

Thomas Flyer Touring, 1906
A similar Flyer, in 1908, won the daring "Race Around the World" from New York to Paris via California and Asia.

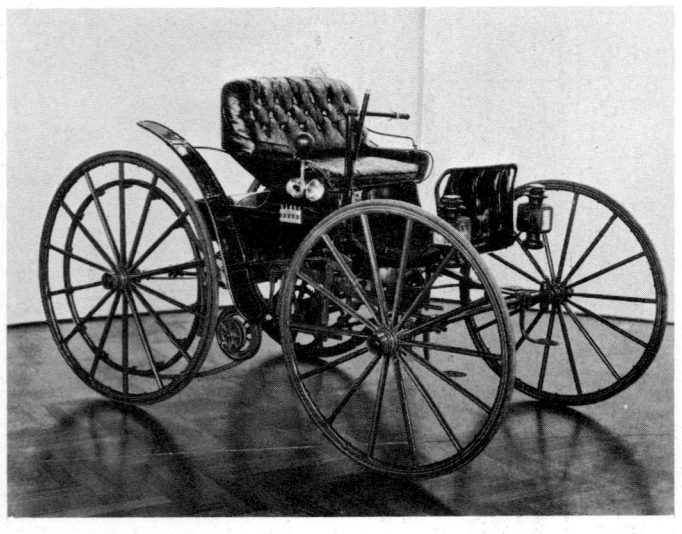

Holsman Auto Buggy, 1903
A motorized buggy with tiller steering and a "rope" drive on pulleys.

Sears Motor Buggy, 1909
In 1909 the mail-order house of Sears, Roebuck & Company offered the Sears Motor Buggy at a cost of $325.

Martini Touring, 1903
Swiss-made with vertical radiator, four-cylinder engine, clutch, transmission, and shaft drive.

Maxwell-Briscoe Junior Runabout, 1911
Featured all-metal bodies, multiple cylinders, and shaft drive.

Above: Henry Ford introduced his famous 1909 Model T as the "Universal Car—rugged, dependable, simple, and low in cost so that nearly everybody can own one." Anxious to prove this claim, Henry Ford entered two cars in the Guggenheim transcontinental endurance race in 1909. The Model T Ford Racer No. 2 came in first in the New York-to-Seattle run, winning out over bigger, heavier, more powerful, and more costly cars. Based on this success, more than fifteen million Model T Fords were ultimately built.

Below: Electric automobiles such as the 1914 Detroit Electric Coupe, personal car of Mrs. Henry Ford, were greatly favored by the ladies, who desired simple, clean, quiet, slow, and sedate personal transportation. The very heavy lead–sulfuric acid batteries, contained in the fore and aft compartments, restricted use of electric cars to paved streets and to short runs of about thirty miles between battery charges. The basic limitations of electric automobiles have still not been overcome despite technological advances.

Above: The famous Rolls-Royce Silver Ghost model, so named for its smooth, quiet-running qualities, was introduced in 1907. Four specially prepared Silver Ghost models, dubbed "Alpine Eagles," were entered as a factory team in the 1913 Austrian Alpine Trials and figuratively flew over the difficult 1,645-mile mountain racecourse to win seven prizes, scoring brilliantly against much larger cars. A single "Eagle," entered by an individual, set a nonstop record in the 1914 Alpine Trials.

Left, center: The five-passenger Ford Model T sedan was fitted with an electric starter and demountable rims in 1919. Thereafter, ladies could drive the Model T without having to crank the engine, and flat tires could easily be changed. This sedan body, first introduced in 1915, was so popular that by 1925 closed cars outsold open-bodied cars in America.

Left, bottom: Edsel Ford received this 1916 Mercer as a wedding gift. Despite the touring body design, Mercer was a real sports car of its day. "Stock" Mercer runabouts were driven to many victories by such famous drivers as Ralph DePalma, Barney Oldfield, and Billy Knipper.

Left: This Chrysler Custom Imperial Landau, appropriate for either chauffeur or owner driving, was designed and built in 1932 especially for Walter P. Chrysler's personal use. In addition to its special aluminum body and high-compression engine, this classic car has many distinctive interior appointments including desk, bar, vanity cases, speedometer, and clock in the rear compartment.

Bottom: This Model A Ford Number One, built on October 21, 1927, with a Tudor body, was personally test driven by Henry Ford before receiving his approval for mass production. It was subsequently fitted with its present Phaeton body, trimmed in leather, and presented to Thomas A. Edison. The Model A, new for 1928, was not a revamped Model T, but so completely original that Henry Ford said, "We are wiping the slate clean and starting all over again with Model A." It is shown parked in front of Edison's Florida *Fort Myers Laboratory,* now at Greenfield Village.

107

The British Rolls-Royce was established as a marque of excellence and opulence by its 1907 Silver Ghost model. In 1926 the six-cylinder Phantom I was introduced. The great American financier, J. P. Morgan, had a limousine body *(above)* custom built by the well-known Brewster & Company of New York and fitted to a 1926 Phantom chassis.

Stutz, famous for "the car that made good in a day," produced between 1911 and 1934 a long line of illustrious champions of road and racecourse. The aptly named Bearcat sports model *(upper right)*, built in 1923, was powered by a four-cylinder, "T" head, dual-ignition engine. Each Bearcat, a glamorous symbol of the flapper-flask-and-raccoon-coat era, was individually tested for performance and speed on the Indianapolis Speedway, scene of its initial successes, before being delivered to the customer.

The 1955 Mercedes 300 SLR race car *(right)*, winner of the 1955 World Championship for Sports Cars, was the last of the great competition models built by Daimler-Benz, A.G., at Stuttgart, Germany. Its eight-cylinder engine, with double overhead camshafts, developed 295 horsepower with a displacement of only 180 cubic inches and drove the car to a speed of 180 miles per hour. The Daimler-Benz racing team was retired from competition when the 300 SLR had proved its excellence beyond doubt.

109

The specially constructed Lincoln limousine *(above)* prepared for President Franklin D. Roosevelt in 1939, was dubbed the "Sunshine Special" because he often rode in it with the top folded down. In 1942, it was returned to the factory and equipped with armor plate and bullet-proof glass, tires, and gas tank for a total weight of nearly five tons. The car was used by President Roosevelt during his historic conferences at Yalta, Casablanca, Teheran, and Malta, and by President Truman until 1950.

This 1940 Crown Imperial Chrysler, specially built and fitted with a handmade Derham body, was used for nearly twenty years in New York City's fabulous official parades and receptions. Its passenger list is a veritable roll-call of the world's dignitaries—kings, ambassadors, statesmen, and notable personages in war, peace, the arts, and the sciences. In the photograph *(right)*, General Dwight D. Eisenhower responds to the excitement of a "ticker-tape parade."

The massive, specially-built 1950 Lincoln convertible was the official car for four Presidents of the United States. It was first used by President Truman *(below)*, then by President Eisenhower who had the plastic "bubble top" *(bottom)* fitted over the tonneau. Presidents Kennedy *(left, bottom)* and Johnson occasionally used it as a second car until its retirement in 1967.

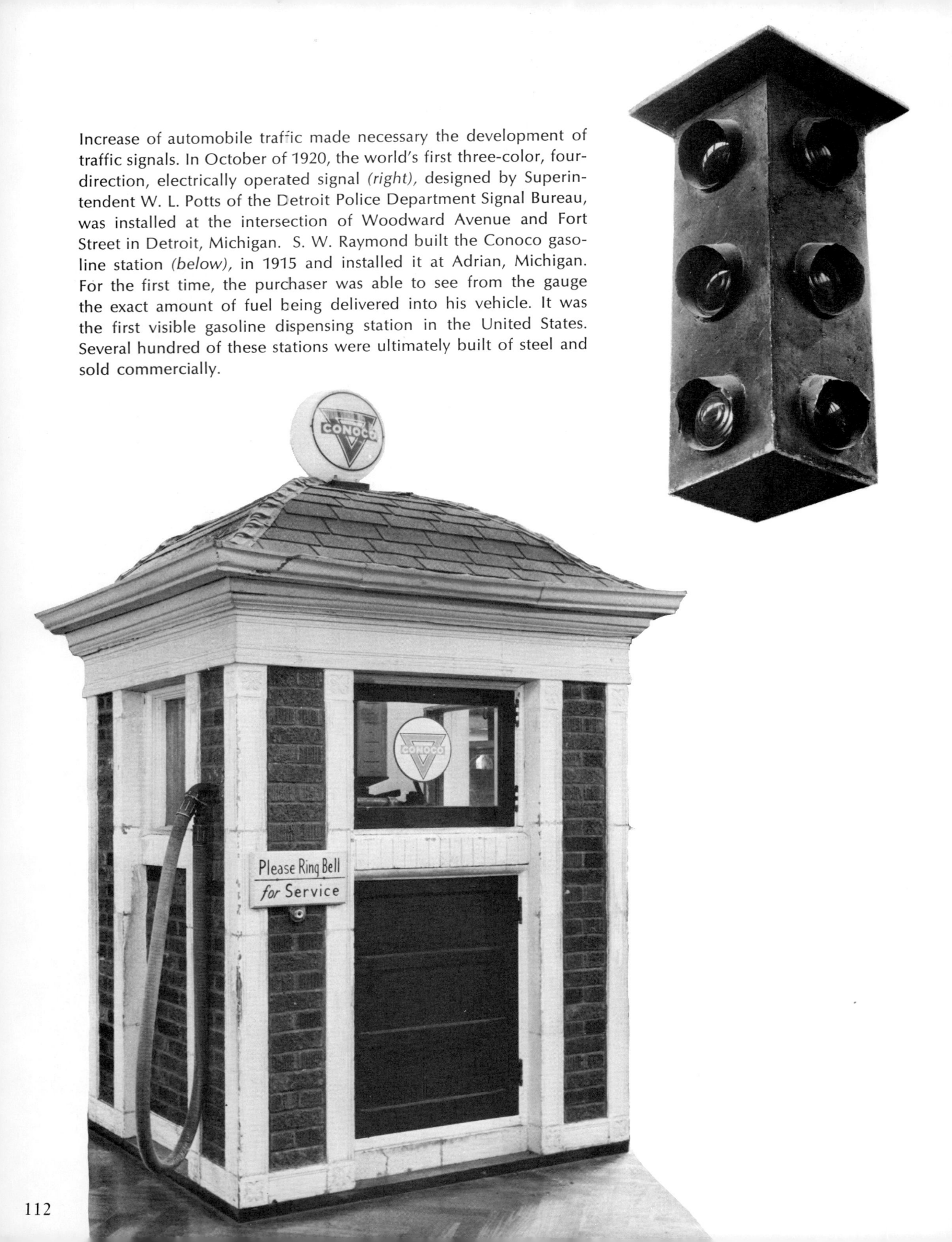

Increase of automobile traffic made necessary the development of traffic signals. In October of 1920, the world's first three-color, four-direction, electrically operated signal *(right)*, designed by Superintendent W. L. Potts of the Detroit Police Department Signal Bureau, was installed at the intersection of Woodward Avenue and Fort Street in Detroit, Michigan. S. W. Raymond built the Conoco gasoline station *(below)*, in 1915 and installed it at Adrian, Michigan. For the first time, the purchaser was able to see from the gauge the exact amount of fuel being delivered into his vehicle. It was the first visible gasoline dispensing station in the United States. Several hundred of these stations were ultimately built of steel and sold commercially.

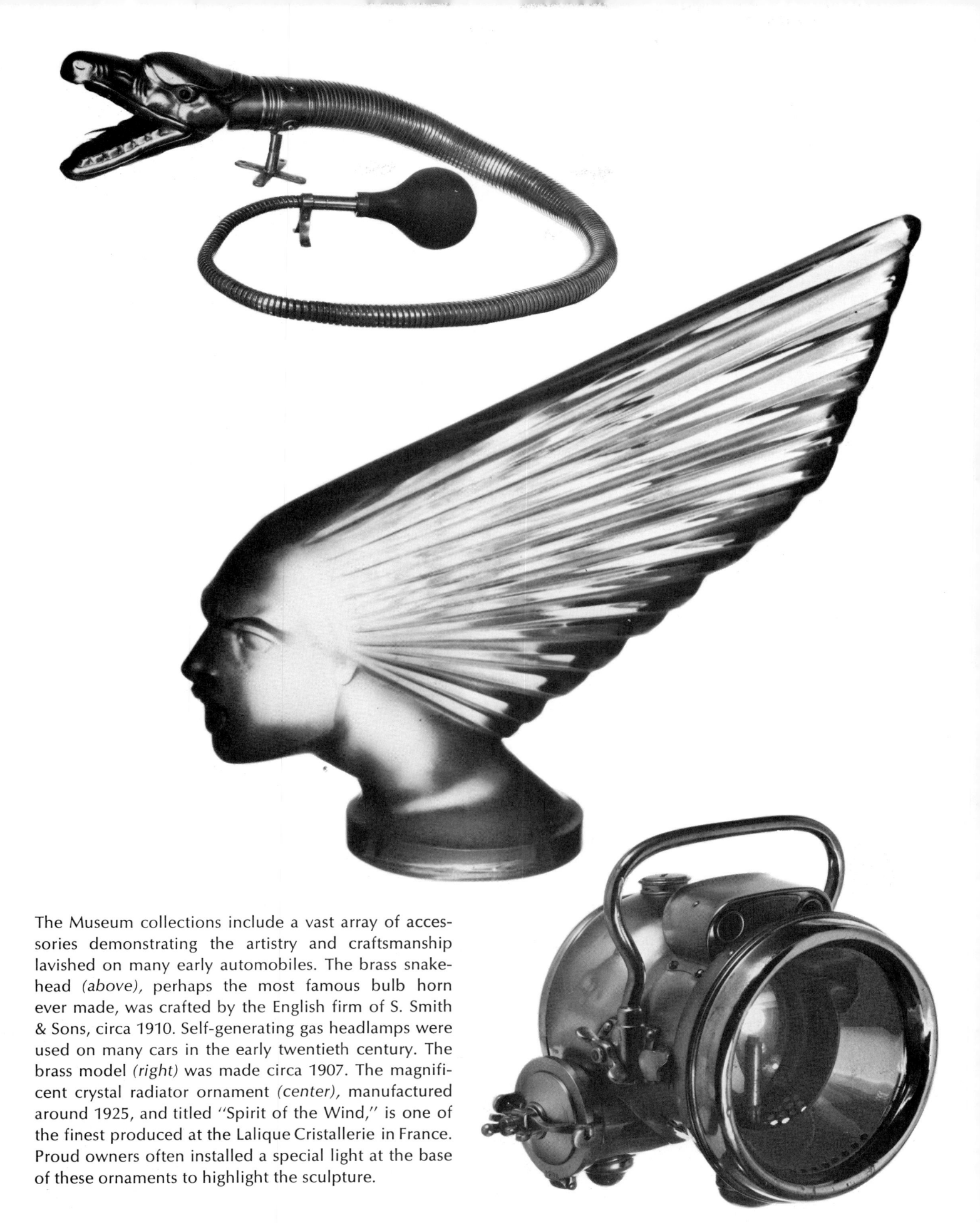

The Museum collections include a vast array of accessories demonstrating the artistry and craftsmanship lavished on many early automobiles. The brass snakehead *(above)*, perhaps the most famous bulb horn ever made, was crafted by the English firm of S. Smith & Sons, circa 1910. Self-generating gas headlamps were used on many cars in the early twentieth century. The brass model *(right)* was made circa 1907. The magnificent crystal radiator ornament *(center)*, manufactured around 1925, and titled "Spirit of the Wind," is one of the finest produced at the Lalique Cristallerie in France. Proud owners often installed a special light at the base of these ornaments to highlight the sculpture.

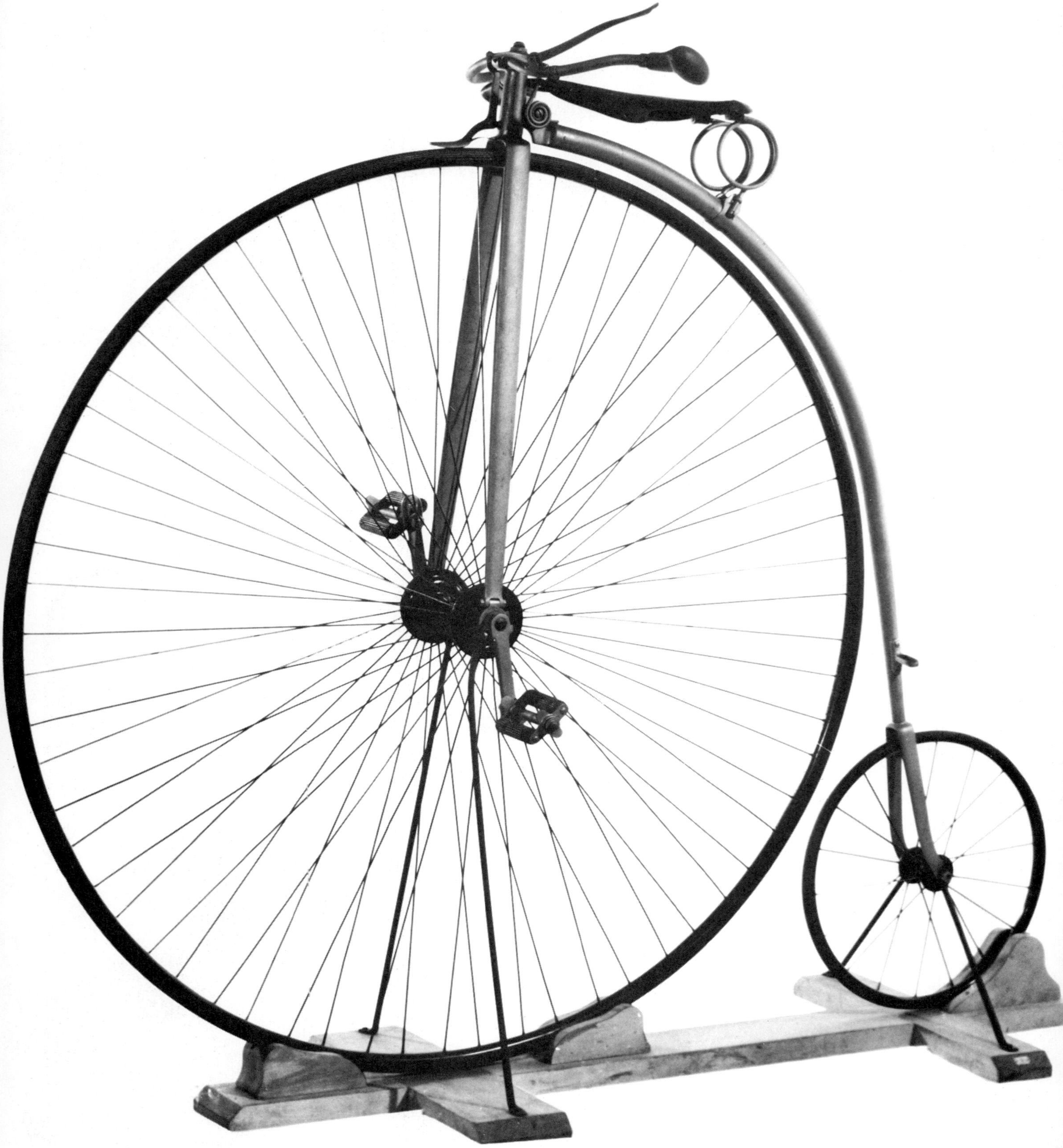

The high-wheel bicycle, transplanted from England to America about 1880, sprang to immediate popularity as a means of personal transportation. Clubs, such as the League of American Wheelmen, promoted improved roads, road signs, and "tourism."

The Columbia high-wheel, or "ordinary," bicycle *(left)* was built in Boston in 1888 by the Pope Manufacturing Company. The size of the large wheel, limited only by the length of a man's legs, determined speed; the small wheel provided a modicum of stability. Pope Manufacturing Company also pioneered in the manufacture of automobiles after 1900.

The ten-man bicycle, "Oriten" *(above)*, is one of the largest in the world. It was built in 1896 as an advertising novelty by the Waltham Manufacturing Company, makers of the famous Orient safety bicycles. Successor to the "ordinary" bicycle, which often pitched its rider over the handlebar onto his head, the safety bicycle had wheels of equal size, pneumatic tires, and chain-and-sprocket drive for speed. Among the most popular was the Rambler *(right)* built in 1892 in Chicago, Illinois, by Gormully & Jeffery Manufacturing Company, inventors of the clincher pneumatic tire. Jeffery began building the Rambler automobile in 1902.

The popularity of motorcycles reached its height shortly after World War I. The 1919 Excelsior 45-cubic inch, twin-cylinder motorcycle *(below)* was originally purchased by Charles A. Lindbergh while he was still in college. Motorcycles are enjoying a revived popularity today.

Though derived from the basic European farm wagon, no horse-drawn vehicle is more typically American, nor more historically significant than the graceful "Conestoga" covered freight wagon *(above)*. It originated in the Conestoga River Valley of the Pennsylvania-Dutch County of Lancaster. Traditionally the wagons were constructed with wide metal-tired wheels for sturdy support. Wagon accessories often included an ornamental toolbox on the side *(left)*, a feed-trough slung on the back, a tallow bucket, a jack, and an ever-handy axe. A later derivation of the Conestoga wagon was the western prairie schooner.

The 1892 horse-drawn tank wagon *(above)* is one of more than six thousand originally used by Standard Oil Company to deliver kerosene for heating and lighting to the farmers in the area between Chicago and Detroit. Early farm tractors and stationary engines also ran on kerosene. As automobiles became more numerous after 1910, many of these wagons were diverted to hauling gasoline and oil to accommodate the new mode of transportation. Horse-drawn wagons, even at this late date, were used instead of motor trucks because they could more easily negotiate the muddy midwestern roadways.

The first commercial truck-trailer *(below)* was produced in 1914 for a 1911 Model T Ford by the Fruehauf Trailer Company, Detroit, Michigan, for use by the Sibley Lumber Company. August C. Fruehauf and Otto Neumann fashioned the trailer in a blacksmith shop on Gratiot Avenue. This was the beginning of the great tractor-trailer industry which Americans depend upon for freight transportation.

One-Horse Shay, circa 1870.

General Lafayette's Phaeton, circa 1820.

Four-Wheel Buggy, 1830.

Until World War I, Americans relied largely on horse-drawn vehicles for transportation. Any travel, other than local, was something of an adventure. Only the wealthy could afford a comfortable, sprung carriage.

Although of European origin, the one-horse, two-wheeled chaise (corrupted to shay) was popular in America because of its low cost, convenience, and adaptability to poor roads. The shay *(left, top)*, suspended by leather through braces on a wooden

Governor's Barouche, 1870.

Phaeton Baby Carriage, circa 1885.

Brougham, 1901–1909.

cantilever spring, was built by Elmer P. Sargent in Merrimac, Massachusetts, for Dr. G. G. Clement of nearby Haverhill.

The Phaeton was a very graceful, light, personal carriage which usually had side panels carved to resemble the shape of a scalloped seashell. It differed from the chaise in that the front wheels prevented the jogging motion of the horse from being transmitted through the shafts to the passenger. The Marquis de Lafayette's personal Phaeton *(far left)* is unique in its three-wheel design. It was brought from France in 1824 on the occasion of his second visit to America. While recuperating from an illness in the Verplanck homestead at Brinckerhoff, New York, he rode daily in the vehicle.

The four-wheeled buggy has long been used by both farmers and townsmen for personal transportation. The light buggy with its high, spindly wheels and end-bar suspension on two transverse, full elliptical steel springs *(far left)*, was built by William C. Fauber in Lebanon, Pennsylvania.

Comfort and elegance are exemplified by the barouche, favorite of wealthy urbanites. The graceful carriage *(near left, top)*, called "The Governor's Coach," was built at a cost of ten thousand dollars by the E. M. Miller Company of Quincy, Illinois, and was used in Nevada for affairs of state. Many celebrities, including Theodore Roosevelt, rode in this carriage. Elegant coachwork is enhanced by the silver door handles and mountings recalling the fabulous bonanza days of early Nevada history.

An opulent baby carriage is a detailed, miniaturized form of the "George IV Phaeton," a vehicle favored by that English monarch.

England's Lord Henry Brougham had a two-passenger, enclosed vehicle built to his specifications so that he could readily enter through a tall door in its drop-center body. This Brougham *(near left, bottom)* was purchased during the administration of President Theodore Roosevelt, and was used by him and succeeding Presidents on official occasions until its retirement in 1928.

In general, the basic design of a horse-drawn carriage was not readily adapted to automotive power. One rare exception is this Roper steam carriage *(below)*, oldest existing and fully operative car in America. It was built in 1863 by Sylvester H. Roper of Roxbury, Massachusetts, and exhibited at country fairs in New England and the Middle West during the 1860s and 1870s. Usually it was pitted against the best trotting horses at the fairs and always won. The car had no brakes; the operator stopped by shutting off the steam to the two-cylinder, oscillating-type engine. Steering was by rack-and-pinion, a design being used in automobiles today. Between 1860 and 1896, Roper built ten steam-powered vehicles including several steam motorcycles.

The horse-drawn fire engine weathervane *(above)* was made by Cushing & White, Waltham, Massachusetts, and dates circa 1875–1900. It is one of many transportation-related vanes in the Folk Art Collection. The steam-pressured pump on this colorful piece relates it to an actual engine *(below)* originally used by the Manchester, New Hampshire, Fire Department. The vertical boiler and combustion chamber was manufactured by the Manchester Locomotive Works and patented on August 8, 1882. The engine was rebuilt in 1900 and put into service by the Detroit Fire Department. The early, leather fireman's hat *(left)*, the brass-trimmed fire belts *(right)*, and the fire hat emblem *(center, bottom)* were standard equipment for early fire-fighters.

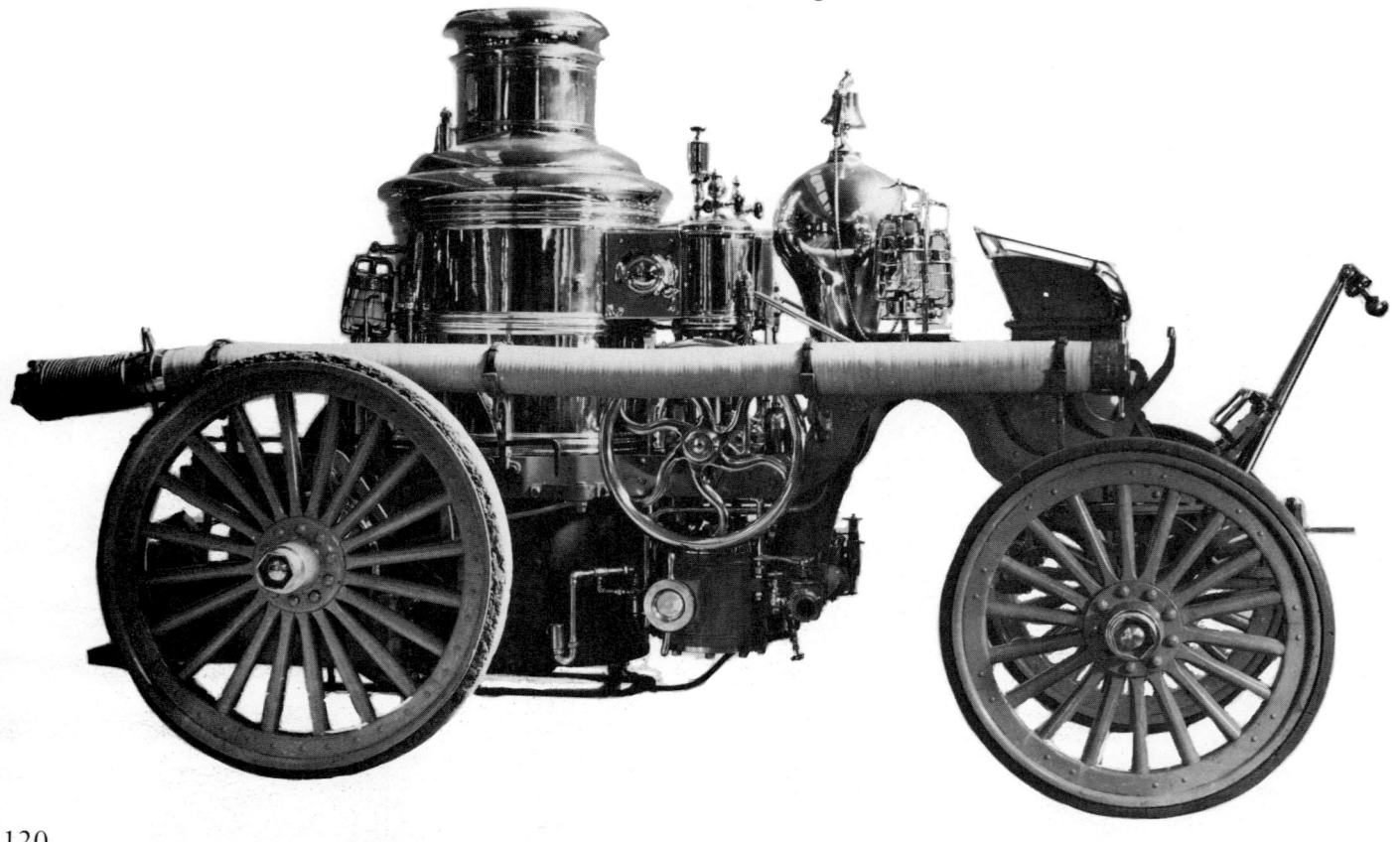

The hand-drawn fire engine *(above)* was manufactured by L. Button & Son at Waterford, New York, in 1873. Volunteer Engine Company #2 of West Newbury, Massachusetts, converted the engine so that it could be horse-drawn. The earliest form of mobile fire fighting equipment was the fire engine *(below)* made by Gleason & Bailey at Seneca Falls, New York, circa 1850. This hand-pump, hand-drawn engine greatly increased firefighter efficiency, replacing the "bucket brigade" with suction hoses that could operate from a nearby stream.

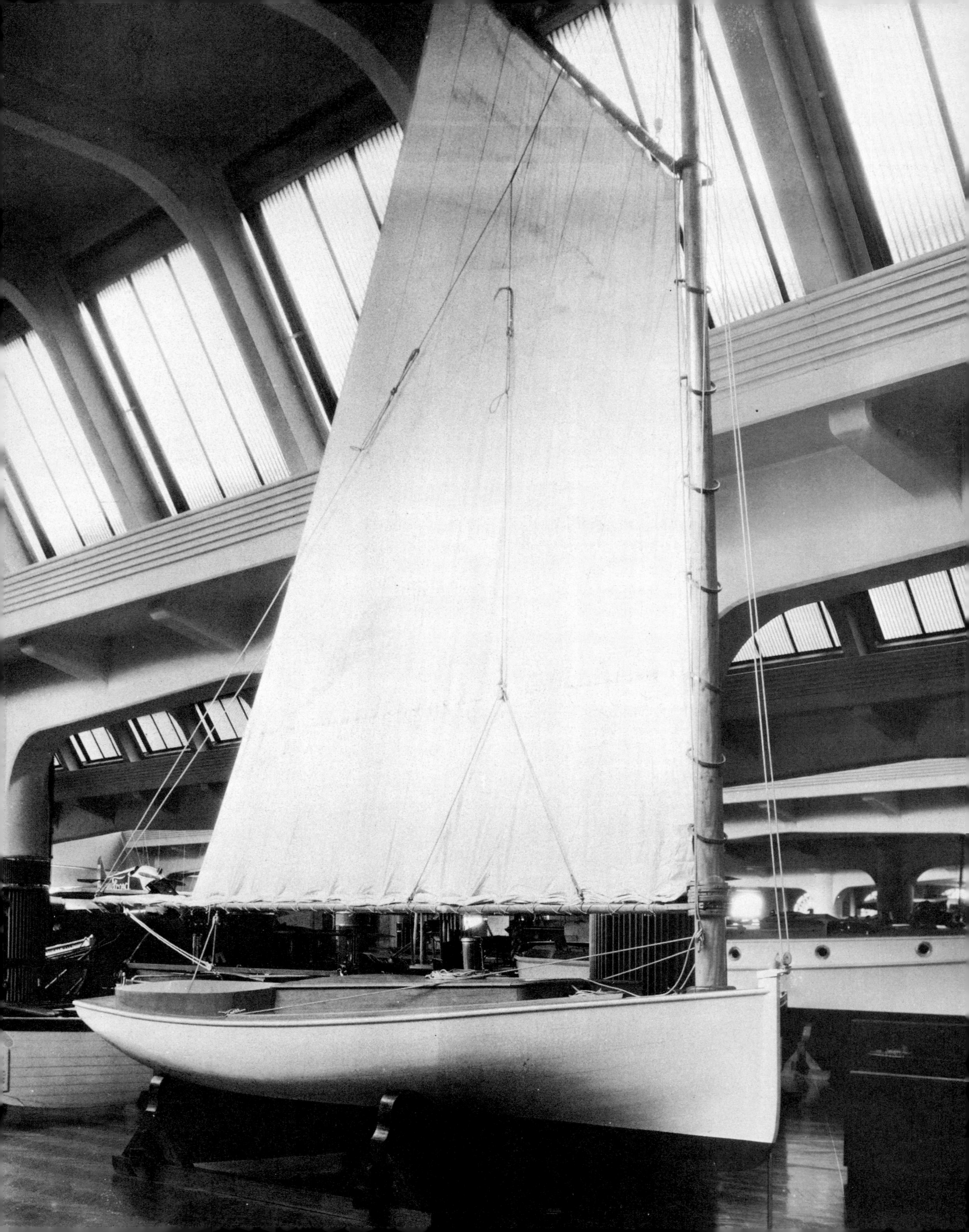

The birchbark canoe *(above)*, a native to America, was adopted as a means of individual transportation by explorers and adventurers. Early commercial travel in America was by wooden sailing vessels, frequently built in New England. The clipper ships of the 1850s represented the epitome of speed in sailing. A Currier and Ives print *(right)* illustrates one of the shipwrights' most beautiful creations—the *Flying Cloud* clipper built by Donald McKay at East Boston, Massachusetts, in 1851. This 1,750-ton, 225-foot vessel still holds the unbroken record of only 89 days sailing out of New York to San Francisco around South America. The small sailboat design called the "catboat" was popular with mid-nineteenth-century sports enthusiasts and is still in limited use today. The 1860 *Sprite (left)* was designed and built by the Herreshoff marine architects at Bristol, Rhode Island.

Early life-saving equipment is rare. This longboat *(right)* with its shore equipment, circa 1870, is marked "Humane Society, Mass." and was last used in 1914 when the barkentine *Beatrice* was stranded on Brass Rip Pass off Nantucket, Massachusetts.

Ore ships, designed especially for use on the Great Lakes, are a vital link in the transportation of materials for the automobile industry. The motorship *Henry Ford II,* built in 1924 by the American Shipbuilding Company at Loraine, Ohio, is represented in the Museum by a 76-inch model *(below)*. She and her sister ship, *Benson Ford,* were for many years the only large diesel-powered ore ships on the Great Lakes.

Steam-powered rail transportation had its inception in England, but attained a high degree of development in America.

One of the earliest locomotives in the collections is the *DeWitt Clinton (left, top)* built by John B. Jervis in 1831 at the West Point Foundry, New York. It was the first train to run in New York State and the third in America. The passenger coaches, built by Gould at Troy, New York, were merely conventional stagecoaches set on flanged iron wheels.

The wood-burning, "American" type locomotive *(left),* built by the Rogers Locomotive Works, Paterson, New Jersey, in 1858, saw service in the Civil War. Restored by Henry Ford and supplied with hand-painted wooden coaches, it was used in the dedication ceremonies of The Edison Institute in 1929.

Streetcars drawn on steel rails by horses provided better, smoother, and slightly faster transportation within cities than the older road coach or omnibus. This coach was built, circa 1881, by the J. M. Jones & Company of West Troy, New York, and used by the Brooklyn Railroad Company until 1897 *(top, center)*.

A manpower shortage brought about by World War I inspired Charles Birney to invent the 1917 "Safety," double-end streetcar *(left),* in which one man served as both conductor and motorman. Used mostly on one-track suburban runs, the operator simply reversed the "trolley" pole, moved to the opposite end of the car, and made the return trip.

The giant six-hundred-ton steam locomotive *Allegheny (below)* was made in Ohio at the Lima Locomotive Works in 1941. It was one of the last and largest coal-burning locomotives built in the United States. Before retirement, it traveled over four hundred thousand miles hauling coal from West Virginia, Virginia, and Kentucky.

124

The local depot, like the general store, was once a focal point of town and village social and business life —a place where American youth could gaze in awe at the mighty "iron horse" and occasionally meet their engineer heroes. This railroad station of the Civil War period is complete with all the equipment used by a stationmaster and train crew.

126

Aviation was born in America in 1903 with the first manned flight by Wilbur and Orville Wright. Six years later, Louis Bleriot, pioneer French airman, made the first flight across the English Channel in his monoplane. A similar Bleriot airplane *(below)* is preserved in the Museum's collection of historic civilian aircraft which also includes two Polar and one Arctic exploration airplanes. Earliest of these is the 1926 Fokker wood-and-fabric, trimotored monoplane *(left, top)* built by Tony Fokker of Holland. Sponsored by Edsel Ford and named *Josephine Ford,* the plane was flown over the North Pole by Admiral Richard E. Byrd in 1926. Three years later, Byrd flew the 1928 all-metal Ford trimotor monoplane *(left, center)* over the South Pole. The Ford trimotor, one of the greatest of all airplanes, is still in commercial use between the Lake Erie islands. It was the first all-metal, multipassenger, multiengine transport airplane; first to make regular, scheduled commercial flights; first to be guided by radio beacon; first to have flight stewards; and first to have "in flight" motion picture shows. The 1929 Lockheed "Vega" *(left, bottom)* is the earliest of its kind extant. Because of its streamlined design, introduced in 1927, and lightweight "monocoque" plywood construction, the "Vega" could attain greater speed than its contemporary transport airplanes. This particular "Vega" was used in 1931 by Arctic explorer Donald MacMillan for mapping Arctic Circle areas and, earlier, as a factory demonstrator, was flown by many aviation "greats" such as Billy Mitchell, Wiley Post, Amelia Earhart, Henry Brown, and Charles A. Lindbergh. The world's first practical helicopter, the Vought-Sikorsky VS-300 *(above)*, established a world's endurance record on September 14, 1939, by staying aloft for 1 hour and 33 minutes. It was flown to the Henry Ford Museum by its designer, Igor Sikorsky, and is now suspended from the ceiling of the huge Mechanical Arts Hall.

1912 Milk Wagon

The horse-drawn milk wagon was one of the most familiar sights in American towns until replaced by the modern dairy truck. Bringing bottled milk at dawn from door to door, it was the successor to the hand cart and wagon of earlier generations of milkmen who measured out milk from cans into the customers' containers.

This wagon, an ample of its type, decorated about 19 lyn, New York Schnabel, wagonm er Schnell, paint by dairyman, Wil Englewood, Ne

IV. Special Exhibitions

Through the presentation of special exhibitions, the Henry Ford Museum fulfills its educational role. Many times each year, objects for an in-depth study of a specific collection are gathered from both the Village and Museum and placed on view in the special exhibition galleries. Traveling shows such as the photographic presentation, "The Family of Man" sponsored by the Museum of Modern Art in New York City, and loan exhibitions like the Henry Ford Museum's thousand-item exhibit, "Midwest Collectors' Choice," are part of the special exhibitions program. The annual "Sports Car Show" *(below)* is presented in an effort to bring to the public a visual demonstration of the more significant steps in the development of our present-day automobile. A dramatic vehicle such as the Bugatti Royale *(above)* never fails to impress, for it was designed to be of such size and elegance that it would shame every other pretentious classic car. "The Gwinn Dairy Exhibition" *(left)*, an astonishing collection of some fifteen hundred objects, books, and documents related to the dairy industry history, celebrates a gift of David M. Gwinn to the agricultural collection begun by Henry Ford.

Each year the Museum sponsors the Midwest Antiques Forum. Focusing on a central theme, *"Collecting Americana,"* world-renowned experts in specific fields of the decorative arts lecture to participants who travel from all parts of the country to attend these informative and popular sessions. A special exhibition relating to the overall theme of the Forum provides a three-dimensional extension of the illustrated lectures. In recent years, "The Craftsmanship of Quality" and "Selected Treasures of the Henry Ford Museum" brought into sharp focus the scope and depth of the Museum's decorative arts collections. The radio *(right)* was featured in an important special presentation, "Talking Box to Telstar," which commemorated the fiftieth anniversary of the broadcasting industry.

"Talking Box to Telstar"

Queen Anne display in "A Decade and a Half of Collecting" Exhibition.

"The Craftsmanship of Quality"

131

The creation of Christmas wreaths, cedar and holly roping, and other traditional decorations is a colorful demonstration given by Museum craftsmen during the holiday season. A woodcarver *(left)* creates toys in the special exhibition, "Crafts at Christmas." A group of room settings in the "Home for Christmas" show *(below)* illustrates how our ancestors celebrated one of their most treasured holidays.

The Clara B. Ford Garden Forum, a three-day annual event at the Henry Ford Museum, is always accompanied by a special exhibition *(right)*. In addition to a full program of illustrated morning and evening lectures, afternoon discussion sessions, and nature walks, participants enjoy the opportunity of conversing with experts and other garden enthusiasts.

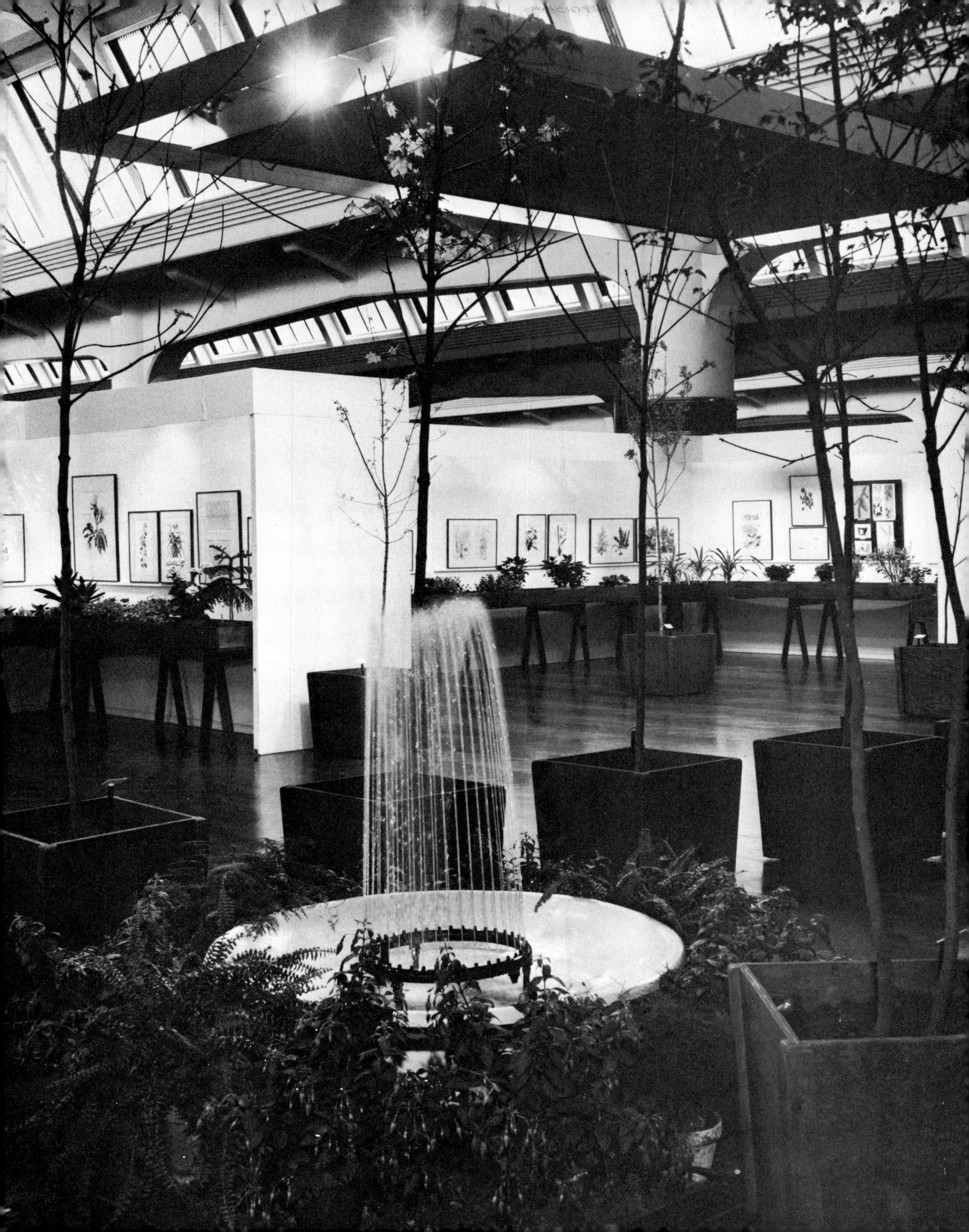

The American Drama Festival, inaugurated in the summer of 1964 at the Henry Ford Museum, presents the Greenfield Village Players—one of the few repertory companies devoted exclusively to the production of early dramas by American playwrights. In addition, it provides facilities for education and instruction in the arts of the theater.

V. American Drama Festival

The American Drama Festival has increased its repertoire from two plays over a six-week period to four plays during a ten-week summer season. Additional performances are given at Christmas and Easter. At other times during the year, the Theater Arts Department presents varied programs of musical concerts, dance recitals, nineteenth-century readings, and early motion pictures. The museum-sponsored Theater Arts Apprentice Program furthers the principle of encouraging talented youth begun by Mr. and Mrs. Henry Ford in their lifetimes. Some of the early plays presented are *Shenandoah,* first performed in 1889; *Rip Van Winkle,* originally produced in 1865; *The Henrietta,* first performed on September 26, 1887; and *Under the Gaslight (below),* which opened on August 12, 1867. During intermission, while the audience sips lemonade under the stars in the torchlit courtyard *(left),* they are serenaded by the actors who then lead them back into the theater for the second half of the performance.

"Industrial Progress, U.S.A.," a traveling exhibit which visited cities across the United States from 1952 through 1955.

"Schoolroom Progress, U.S.A.," a traveling display contrasting early American schools with the latest equipment of the 1950s.

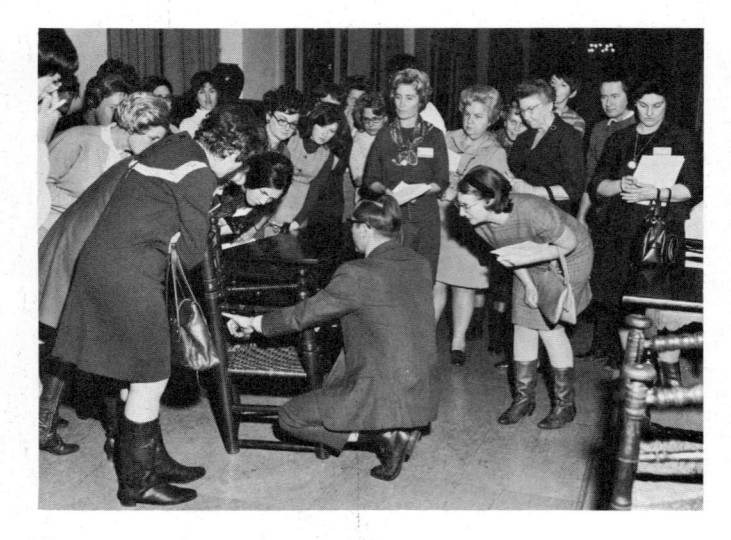

Adult Education classes: Rug Hooking and the History of American Furniture.

VI. Educational Activities

The Adult Education Division provides an opportunity to become better acquainted with early American artifacts and culture. Collections at the Museum and Village serve as teaching aids in a series of enrichment courses taught by members of the Museum's professional staff. Subjects offered are American furniture, clocks, glass, metals, automobiles, the rifle, and decorating with antiques.

Instruction in various early American crafts include glassblowing, dried flower arranging, spinning, weaving, pottery-making, metalworking, and chair-caning.

In conjunction with the University of Michigan, the Museum offers a two-year graduate program leading to a Master of Museum Practice degree. A joint effort with the Adult Education Division of Wayne State University and the Michigan State University coordinates graduate courses with workshops for teachers. The Division also works with individual professors at a number of Michigan colleges to arrange short sessions utilizing the Museum and Village in a variety of academic fields. The Adult Education Division, with other facilities, is housed in the Education Building. On the second floor of this structure is *Lovett Hall (below)*, a grand ballroom named for Benjamin B. Lovett, the dancing master Mr. Ford brought from Massachusetts to teach early American dancing.

VII.
Museum Research Library

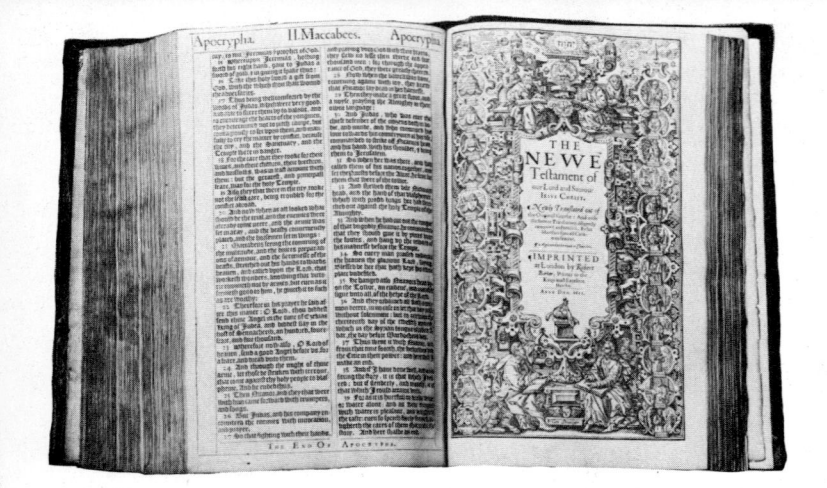

The Library of the Henry Ford Museum is one of the great research centers for scholars of American history. Over two hundred thousand books, pamphlets, periodicals, and ephemeral items in the reference section are devoted to all phases of Americana. The rare book and manuscript collections contain treasures which offer original background and source material relating to the United States from its Colonial days to the present. Pilgrim settlers probably brought with them copies of a 1611 translated Bible now known as the King James Version *(above)*. The self-portrait by John Watson (1685–1768) *(near right)*, the watercolor "Profile of the Carriage of George Washington" *(below, left)*, Washington's bookplate *(below, right)*, and the 1779 State of Massachusetts Bay Lottery Certificate *(far right, bottom)*, along with holograph letters and important historic documents relating to early political and military leaders, vividly portray the American story. An integral part of the Library is the map collection. A sixteenth-century map by Sebastian Munster *(far right, top)* was the first to depict the American continent. Other maps illustrate sections of the country, states, and plans of cities and forts.

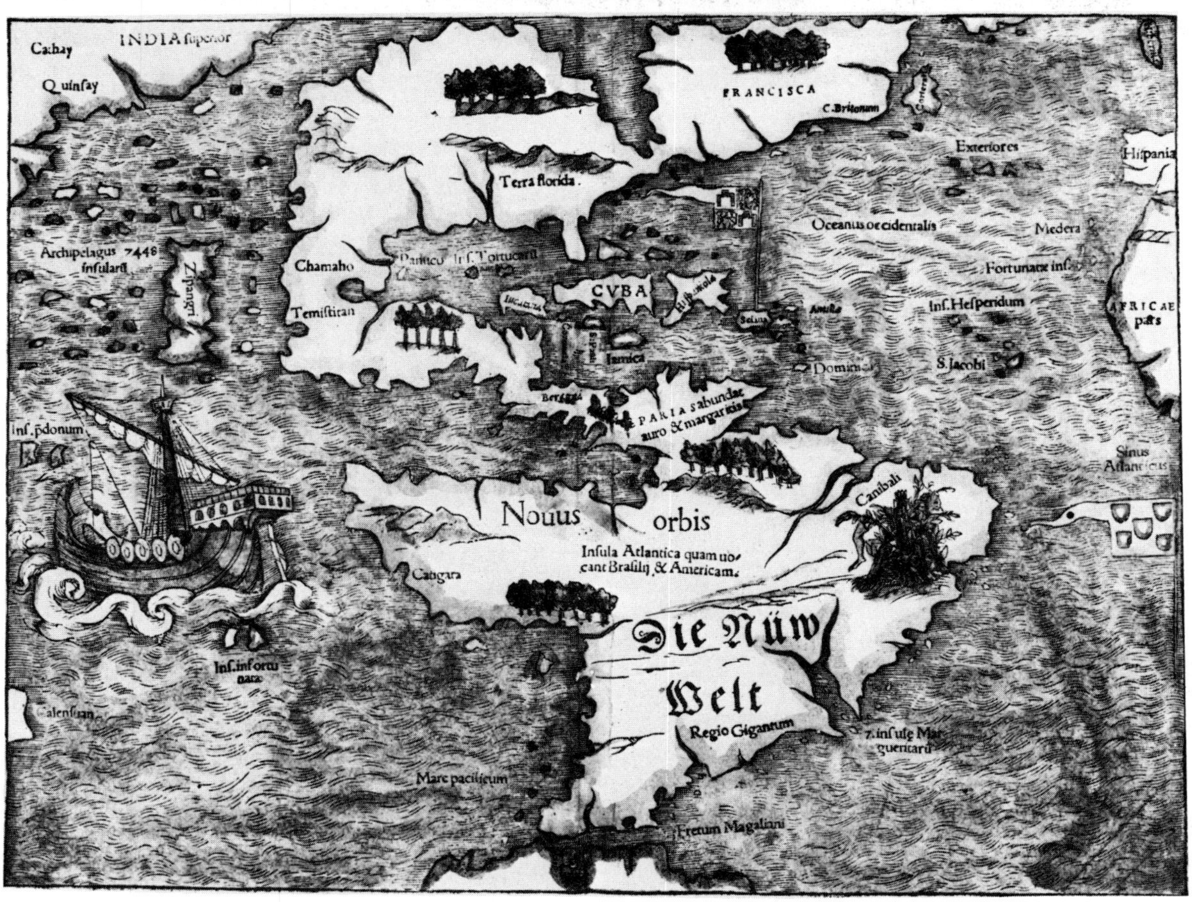

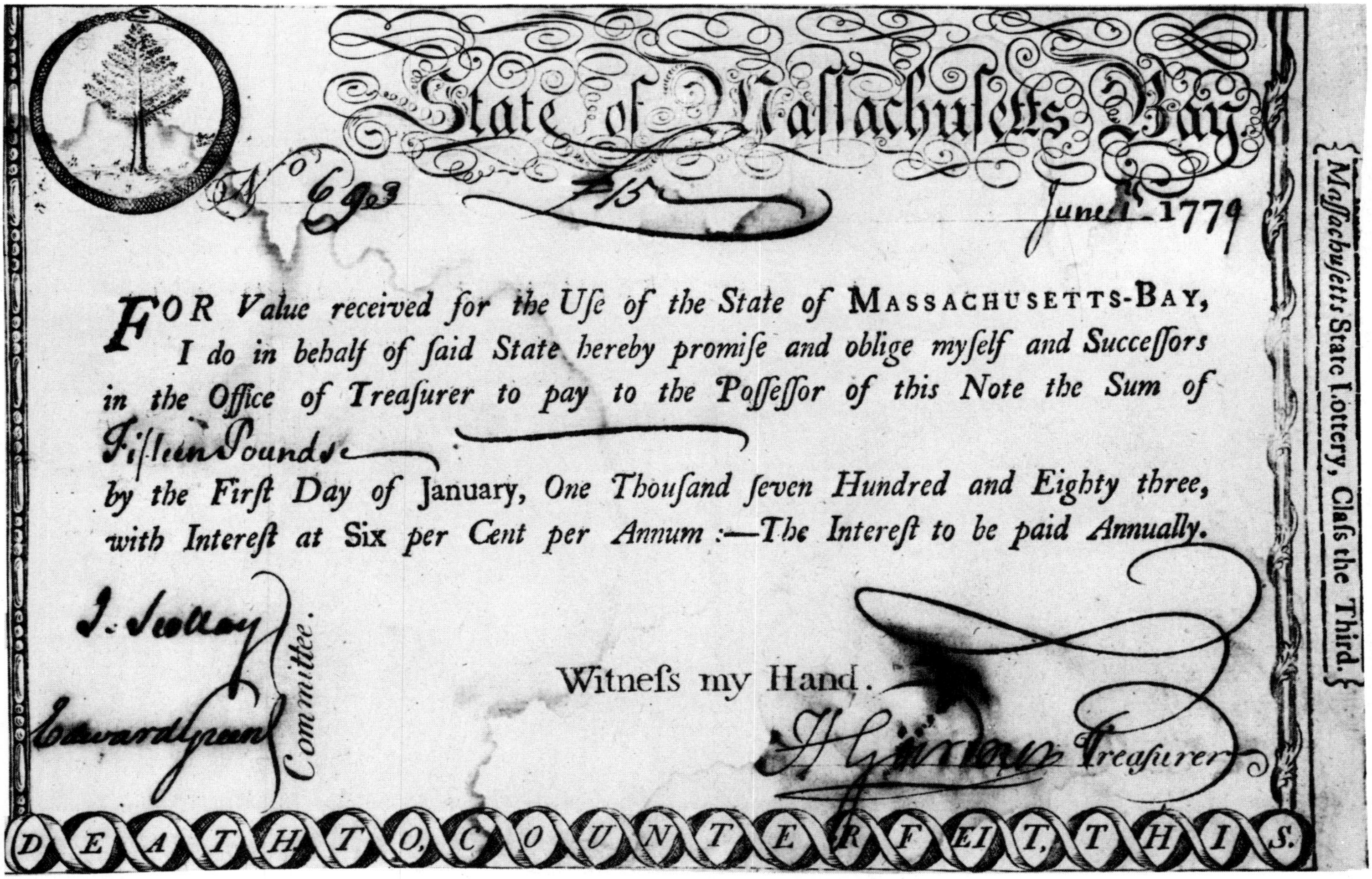
State of Massachusetts Bay

No 6903 £15 June 1st 1779

FOR Value received for the Use of the State of MASSACHUSETTS-BAY, I do in behalf of said State hereby promise and oblige myself and Successors in the Office of Treasurer to pay to the Possessor of this Note the Sum of Fifteen Pounds — by the First Day of January, One Thousand seven Hundred and Eighty three, with Interest at Six per Cent per Annum :—The Interest to be paid Annually.

J. Scollay
Edward Green
Committee.

Witness my Hand.

H Gardner Treasurer

Massachusetts State Lottery, Class the Third.

DEATH TO COUNTERFEIT THIS.

The Bloody Massacre (left), an event which took place in Boston, Massachusetts, on March 5, 1770, and which sparked the American Revolution, was engraved, printed, and sold by Paul Revere. The Museum's copy is one of two known which were hand-colored and signed by Christian Remich. Military engagements were always a popular subject. The Currier and Ives print, published in 1862 *(right, bottom)*, shows the *Battle of Fredericksburg*, Virginia, in December 1862 during the Civil War.

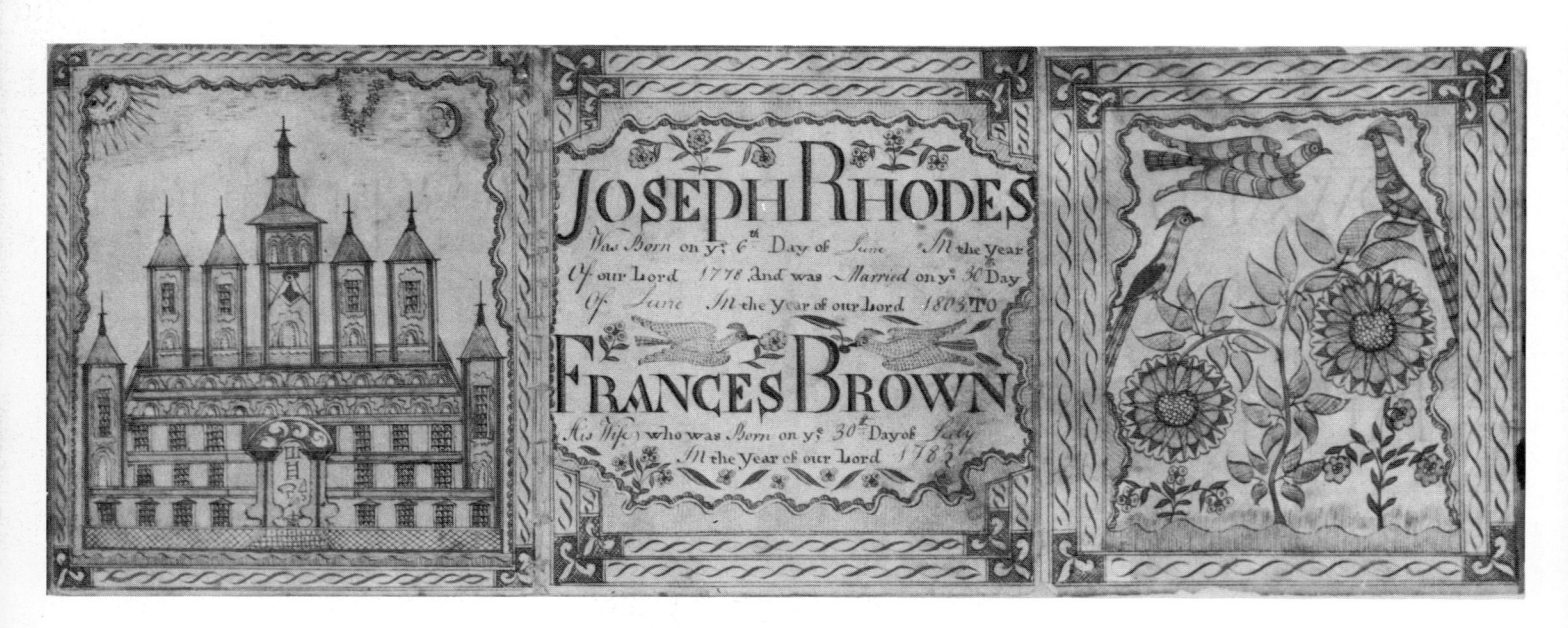

Represented in the print collection are all of the outstanding American printmakers including Peter Pelham, Paul Revere, Nathaniel Hurd, Amos Doolittle, Currier and Ives, Louis Prang, and the Kelloggs. *Osceola*, a colorful Seminole leader, is shown before Indian tents proudly displaying his rifle in an 1842 lithograph published by Daniel Rice and James G. Clark of Philadelphia, Pennsylvania. It was drawn, printed, and colored at J. T. Bowen's Lithographic Establishment. The painted fraktur by John Barnard *(far left, bottom)* is probably from Ohio, circa 1803, and represents a relatively large group of such pieces executed by the artist. The libraries contained within original buildings in nearby Greenfield Village are, for the most part, associated with the famous owners such as Thomas Alva Edison's books, manuscripts, and papers in the Menlo Park buildings, the personal books in the Wright brothers' home, and the Luther Burbank office collection. The library in the Joseph Pearson *Secretary House* matches an original inventory of the house taken in 1823. One of the most treasured groups of books in the Museum Library is a collection of all editions of McGuffey Readers, assembled by Mr. and Mrs. Henry Ford in 1914. This was their first collecting effort and the one which ultimately led to their founding The Edison Institute.

BATTLE OF FREDERICKSBURG, V*ª* DEC. 13TH 1862.

This battle shows with what undaunted courage, the Lion-hearted Army of the Potomac always meets its foes.— After forcing the passage of the Rappahannock on the 11th in the face of a murderous fire from concealed Rebels, and taking possession of Fredericksburg on the 12th, on the morning of the 13th the Army rushed with desperate valor on the intrenchments of the enemy, and thousands of its dead and dying, tell of the fearful strife which raged till night put an end to the carnage. Though driven back by an intrenched and hidden foe, the Soldiers of the North are still as ready to meet the Traitors of the South, as in their days of proudest victory.

Left: Henry Ford's personal holdings of capital stock in the Ford Motor Company in 1903 were 255 shares.

VIII. Ford Archives

The Ford Archives, presented to The Edison Institute in 1964, are housed in the Henry Ford Museum. They are the largest collection of records known that relate to a single individual, his family, his broad personal interests, his philanthropic achievements, and the worldwide business he founded. Fourteen million documents, books, and manuscripts and some four hundred fifty thousand original photographic negatives form this rich, significant research collection that extends virtually to the present day. It is also the most comprehensive non-governmental resource covering American personalities and events of the first half of the twentieth century. These unique, comparatively unpublished materials are readily available to qualified scholars and historians.

On the second floor of the Museum, a permanent exhibition, entitled "Henry Ford, A Personal History," is dedicated to the memory of the man whose creative influence reshaped today's world. The elements of his daily life, his first homemade tools, and the many honors and gifts that later came to him in recognition of his accomplishments have all been carefully selected and arranged to tell the success story of Henry Ford's rise from a Dearborn farm boy to a genius of world renown.

Left: Henry Ford and the Quadricycle, his first gasoline-powered vehicle, on the streets of Detroit, Michigan, in October, 1896.

Below: Ford developed his first gasoline engine on the kitchen sink of his home at 58 Bagley Avenue, Detroit, Michigan. Mrs. Ford kept the engine running by supplying it with gasoline from a medicine dropper.

143

On April 1, 1913, Henry Ford began using his newly developed moving assembly line at the Highland Park, Michigan, plant. Through the installation of such innovative concepts as the body drop *(below)*, production was increased from seventy-five thousand to three hundred thousand cars a year.

The Ford Model T was first produced in 1908. In May of 1927, the fifteen millionth and last of this model *(left)* came off the assembly line.

Ford's oak-paneled Highland Park office was the center of the Ford industry. The Museum exhibit *(bottom)* is a full-scale installation using the original paneling and office furniture.

Bottom: Nothing better illustrates the diversity of Henry Ford's mind than his many friends and acquaintances from all walks of life. He was the friend-in-common who united three seemingly different individuals—the tire manufacturer Harvey Firestone, Sr., the inventor Thomas Alva Edison, and the naturalist John Burroughs. These men, calling themselves the "Four Vagabonds," traveled from the Florida Everglades to Michigan's Upper Peninsula searching for unspoiled forest areas where they could enjoy outdoor life. In 1921, Warren G. Harding, President of the United States, joined the group for a rustic banquet and dined with them at the large folding table that is now featured in the Personal History display.

Center: The opening of the 1939 New York World's Fair was attended by dignitaries from the world over. Participating in the dedication ceremonies were Grover Whalen, Henry Ford II, Edsel Ford, Henry Ford, Alfred E. Smith, and Fiorello La Guardia.

Above: Henry Ford's three grandsons, Benson, Henry Ford II, and William Clay, have followed the footsteps of their grandfather and their father, Edsel Ford, in the preservation of America's heritage. Serving for many years as members of the Board of Trustees, with William Clay as Chairman, they are continuing to further the development of The Edison Institute.

Index

Page numbers in *italics* indicate an illustration.

A

Adam, Robert (1728–92), 20
Adams, Abigail (1744–1818), 46
Adult Education classes, 136, 137
Affleck, Thomas (1740–95), 10, 31
Agriculture, 74, 75, 129
Airplanes, 101, *126*, 127
Allegheny (locomotive), 124
Amelung, Frederick (1739–98), 49
American Coverlets exhibition, 62, *63*
American Drama Festival, 134, 135
American Shipbuilding Co., 123
Ames, "Judge" J. Judson, 93
Andrew, J. E. H., 88
Anthony, Joseph, Jr. (1762–1814), 32
Apostle spoons, 32
Archer Manufacturing Company, 69
Association of Licensed Automobile Manufacturers, 102
Atmospheric engines, 87, 88
Automobile accessories, 113
Automobiles, *100*–108, *109*, 115, 117, 119, 129, 137

B

Bacon, Irving R. (working 1930–45), 10
Badger, Joseph (1708–65), 38
Bagley Avenue, No. 58, 143
Barber, Ralph (1869–1936), 51
Barnard, John (working c. 1810), 141
Barnhart, John, 22
Barry, Joseph B., & Sons, 24
Barton, William (working c. 1825), 37
Bassett, Francis, I (1690–1758), 59
Bassett, Frederick (1761–1800), 59
Battle of Fredericksburg, 140, *141*
Bell, John (1826–81), 67
Belleek porcelain, 45
Belter, John Henry (1804–63), 27
Benbridge, Henry (1744–1812), 39
Benson Ford (Great Lakes freighter), 123
Best and Russell, 37
Betty lamps, 80
Bevan, Edward, 93
Bible, King James version, 138
Bicycles, 101, *114*, 115
Birney, Charles, 124
Blake, Philos, 83
Bleriot, Louis (1872–1936), 127
Bleriot monoplane, 127
Bloody Massacre, The, 140
Boardman, Thomas Danforth, & Co. (active 1805–50), 37
Boats, 97, 101, *122*, 123

Boelen, Jacob, II (1733–86), 34
Boss washing machine, 79
Boston and Sandwich Glass Company, 49, 51, 84
Boulton, Matthew (1728–1809), 88
Bowens, J. T., Lithographic Establishment, 141
Bradley, Isabelle, Millinery Shop, 62
Brewster, William (1567–1644), 14
Brewster & Company, 108
Bridges, Charles (working 1735–40), 39
Bright, George (1726–1805), 20
Brooklyn Railroad Company, 124
Brougham, Lord (1778–1868), 119
Brown, C. H. (working 1870–80), 88
Brown, Gawen (1719–1801), 31
Brown, Henry, 127
Brown, J. C., 31
Brown, John F., Gun & Locksmith Shop, 70
Buehler, Colonel C. H., 57
Bugatti Royale, 129
Burbank, Luther (1849–1926), 8
  garden office, 141
Burroughs, John (1837–1921), 145
Button, L., & Son, 121
Byrd, Admiral Richard E. (1888–1957), 127

C

Cadillac Runabout, 104
Cameras, 92
Canadochly Lutheran Church, 36
Card, H., Turner & Carver Shop, 61
Carriages, 101, 118, 119
Case, J. I., Company, 76
Certificate, Lottery, State of Massachusetts Bay, 138, *139*
Certificate, Stock, Ford Motor Company, 143
Chambers Colliery, 87
Chapple, William, 70
Chicago World's Fair, 14
Chippendale, Thomas (c. 1718–79), 19
Christmas, 132
Chrysler, Walter P. (1875–1940), 107
Chrysler automobiles, 107, 110
Clara B. Ford Garden Forum, 132, *133*
Clement, Dr. G. G., 118
Clinton, De Witt (1769–1828), 39
Clocks, *30*, 31, 37
Columbia, S. S. (steamship), 97
Columbian printing press, 93
Communications, 92, *93*, 94, 95, 98, *99*
Conoco gasoline delivery station, 112

147

Cooper, J. (1695–1754?), 39
Cornelius, Robert, 83
Cornelius & Co. (active c. 1843), 83
Corner Drug Store, *55*
Cornerstone at Henry Ford Museum, 8, 10
Coults, Abigail Matson, 35
Crafts, 58, 67, 132, 137
Crafts at Christmas, 132
"Craftsmanship of Quality," 130, *131*
Crossley Brothers, 88
Cummings, Thomas Seir (1804–94), 39
Currier and Ives, 40, 123, 140
Cushing and White, 120
Cutler, David, Pewter Shop, 58

D
Daguerre, Louis J. M. (1789–1851), 92
Daimler-Benz, 98
Danforth family, 37
Davis, Theodore (working 1879), 47
Dearborn, General Henry (1751–1829), 39
DeBisschop, A., 88
Declaration of Independence, 5, 29
Defibaugh, David, 70
Delft pottery, *16, 17,* 64
De Palma, Ralph (1887–1956), 106
Derr, Peter (1793–1868), 80
Detroit Electric Coupe, 105
Detroit Fire Department, 120
De Witt Clinton (locomotive), 124
Domestic arts, 78, 79
Doolittle, Amos (1754–1832), 141
Dramas, 134, *135*
Dugliss, Hosea (working 1798–1820), 19
Duncan, John, 39
Duyckinck, Gerardus, Sr. (1695–1746?), 17
Duyckinck, Gerret (1660–c. 1710), 39

E
Earhart, Amelia (1898–1937), 127
Earl, Ralph (1751–1801), 39
Earle, James (1734–1810), *38,* 39
Edison, Thomas Alva (1847–1931), 8, 10, 80, 92, 95, 97, 98, 107, 141
Edison Institute, The, 124, 141
Edison Machine Works, 97
Education Building, 137
Eisenhower, Dwight D. (1890–1969), 47, *110, 111*
Electric converters, 97
Electrostatic Machine, 96
Esmeralda Star, 93
Evans, Oliver (1755–1819), 87

F
"Fair Lane," 84
"Family of Man, The," 129
Fanning mill, 76
Fauber, William C., 119
Ferguson, Thomas Ladson, *38,* 39
Field, Robert (c. 1770–1819), 39

Firearms, 5, 70, *71,* 137
Fire fighting equipment, 120, 121
Firestone, Harvey, Sr. (1868–1938), 145
Fishkill Landing Machine Company, 77
Flail, 76
Flying Cloud, 123
Fokker monoplane, *126,* 127
Ford, Benson (1919–   ), 145
Ford, Clara B. (1866–1950), 84, 105, 132, 135, 141, 143
Ford, Edsel (1893–1943), 54, 106, 127, 145
Ford, Henry (1863–1947), 2, 8, 10, 14, 77, 80, 84, 101, 102, 103, 107, 129, 135, 141, *142,* 143, 145
Ford, Henry, II (1917–   ), 145
Ford, William Clay (1925–   ), 145
Ford Archives, *142, 143, 144, 145*
Ford Model A, 2, 102, 107
Ford Model T, 2, *3,* 105, 106, 107, 117, 145
Ford Motor Company, 2, *3,* 143, 144, *145*
Ford "999" race car, 103
Ford trimotor monoplane, *126,* 127
Forestville Manufacturing Co., 31
Fort Myers, Florida, Laboratory, 107
Fowle, Samuel F., 34
Fowler, Charles, Barber Shop, 69
Frakturs, *140,* 141
Franklin, Benjamin (1706–90), 14, 17, 29, 40, *41,* 62
Franklin, Maria (d. 1818), 39
Fraser, Charles (1782–1860), 39
Fruehauf, August C. (1867–1930), 117
Fruehauf Trailer Company, 117
Furniture
    Chippendale, 10, 14, *18,* 19, 31
    Classical Revival, 14, 24
    Country, 14
    Empire, 14, 24, *25,* 137
    English, 14
    Federal, 14, 20, *21, 22,* 23
    Late Classical, 27
    Queen Anne, 14, 17, 31, 43, *131*
    Renaissance Revival, 27
    Rococo Revival, 27
    seventeenth century, 14, *15*
    Shaker, 28, *29, 30,* 31
    Victorian, 14, *26,* 27, 69
    Windsor, 29
    Zoarite, 28, *29*
Fussell, Solomon (1700–62), 17

G
Gansevoort, General Peter (1749–1812), 70
Gardens, 132, *133*
General Electric Company, 97
Generators, 96, 97
Gernsback, Hugo, 95
Gettysburg Blues, The, 56, *57*
Gibson & Davis (active 1801–20), 22
Girl Coming Through Doorway, 37
Glass, *48–51,* 84, 113, 137

Glassblowing, 137
Gleason & Bailey, 121
Gold, 34, *35*
Gormully & Jeffery Manufacturing Co., 115
Grain cradle, 75
Grain drill, 75
Grant, Ulysses S. (1822–85), 14, 40, *41*, 47
Grease lamps, 80, *81*
Greenfield Village Players, 134, *135*
Guggenheim Transcontinental Race, 105
Gurdlestone & Son, East India Merchants Shop, 54
"Gwinn Dairy Exhibition," *128*, 129

H
Hadley's Toy Shop, 54, *55*
Haggerty Power Plant, 67
Hancock, John (1736/7–93), 14
Harding, Chester (1792–1866), 39
Harding, Warren G. (1865–1923), 145
Harrisburg Glass Works, 49
Harrows, 74
Haviland china, 47
Hayes, Rutherford B. (1822–93), 47
Henrietta, The (play), 135
Henry Ford Museum, map of, *12-13*
Henry Ford II (Great Lakes freighter), 123
Hepplewhite, George (d. 1786), 20
Hermitage, The, 24
Herreshoff marine architects, 123
Heyne, Johann Christoph (1715–81), 36
Hoe, R., Company, 93
Holsman Auto Buggy, 104
Holtz, Elizabeth (1734–58), 34
Hollingshead, William (working 1754–85), 32
Hoover, Herbert (1874–1964), 8
Houdon, Jean Antoine (1741–1828), 40
Howe Dye Works, 88
Humane Society, Mass., lifesaving boat, 123
Hunting, Mr. Morgan, *56*, 57
Hurd, Nathaniel (1730–77), 141
Hussey, Obed (1792–1860), 55

I
Incandescent lamp, 8, 10, 97
Independence Hall, 8, *9*, 10
"Industrial Progress," 136
Internal combustion engine, 88

J
Jackson, Andrew (1767–1845), 24
Jarves, Deming (1790–1869), 51
Jarvis, John Wesley (1780–1840), 39
Jefferson, Thomas (1743–1826), 29
Jenkins, C. Francis (1867–1934), 98
Jervis, John B. (1795–1885), 124
Jewel Coal Saving Range, 79
Jewelry, 34, 35
Jigsaw, 91

Johnson, Lyndon B. (1908–), 111
Jones, J. M., & Company, 124
Josephine Ford (airplane), *126*, 127

K
Kellogg Brothers, Printmakers, 141
Kennedy, John F. (1917–63), 47, *110*, 111
Kip, Jesse (1660–1722), 32
Knipper, Billy, 106
Knowles, Taylor & Knowles, 45

L
Lafayette, Marquis de (1757–1834), 119
La Guardia, Fiorello (1882–1947), 145
Lalique Cristallerie, 113
Langen, Eugene (1833–95), 88
Lard oil lamps, *82*, 83
Lathes, 90, 91
Lawrence, William S. (working c. 1834), 83
League of American Wheelmen, 115
Lee, H., and Le Brun, E., 94
Lee, Richard, Jr. (1775–c. 1830), 37
Lee, Richard, Sr. (1747–1823), 37
Leland, Henry M. (1843–1932), 104
Lenox china, 46, 47
Library, Henry Ford Museum, 138
Lifesaving equipment, 123
Lighting, 80, 81, *82*, 83, 84, *85*
Lima Locomotive Works, 124
Lincoln, Abraham (1809–65), 14, 27, 40, *141*, 147
Lincoln automobiles, 110, 111
Lind, Jenny (1820–87), 62
Lindbergh, Charles A. (1902–), 101, 115, 117
Lockheed "Vega" (airplane), *126*, 127
Locomotives, 1, 101, 103, 124
Longfellow, Henry Wadsworth (1807–82), 32
Lovett, Benjamin B., 137
Lovett Hall, 137
Lownes, Joseph (working 1780–1816), 32

M
Machinery, 90, 91, 96
MacMillan, Donald (1874–1970), 127
Malbone, Edward Greene (1777–1807), 39
Manchester Locomotive Works, 120
Mantua Glass Works, 49
Maps, 138, *139*
Mariatta Steam Mill Company, *86*, 87
Mark, George Washington (1795–1879), 57
Martini Touring (automobile), 104
Masonic jewels, 34
Maudslay, Henry (1771–1831), 91
Maxwell-Briscoe Junior Runabout, 104
McAllister, James (working 1840–50), 34
McCormick, Cyrus (1809–84), 55
McGuffey Reader, *140*, 141
McIlworth, Thomas (working 1757–67), 39
McIntire, Samuel (1757–1811), 24

McKay, Donald (1810–80), 123
McNamee, Graham (1889–1942), 8
Menlo Park Compound, 8, 141
Mercedes 300 SLR race car, 108, *109*
Mercer automobile, 106
Metals, 32–37, 59, 79, 80, 83, 113, 137
Meters, *96*, 97
Michigan State University, 137
Midwest Antiques Forum, 130, *131*
"Midwest Collectors Choice," 129
Miller, D. D. (active c. 1852), 83
Miller, E. M., Company, 118
Miss Huysche, *38*, 39
Mitchell, William "Billy" (1879–1936), 127
Moore, William, 40
Morgan, J. P., Jr. (1868–1943), 108
Morse, Samuel F. B. (1791–1872), 92
Motorcycles, 101, 115, 119
Mounts, Aaron (1873–1949), 54
Munster, Sebastian (1489–1552), 138
Museum of Modern Art, 129
Mutzer, Frederick (working c. 1835), 49

N
Neumann, Otto, 117
Newcomen, Thomas (1663–1729), 87
New England Glass Company, 49
Norton, Thomas (working c. 1800), 31
Noyes Comb Shop, *68*, 69

O
Oldfield, Barney (1878–1946), 103, 106
Oliver Company, 74
Optical Scanner, 98, *99*
"Oriten" bicycle, 115
Osborn, D. M., & Company, 55
Osceola (c. 1800–38), 141
Otto, Nicholas (1832–91), 88

P
Paintings, *10*, *38*, 39, 40, *56*, 57
Paperweights, 51
Peale, Anna Claypoole (1791–1878), 39
Peale, Charles Willson (1741–1827), 39
Pelham, Peter (c. 1695–1751), 141
Pewter, 36, 37, 59, *62*, 63
Phillips, Ammi (1787–1865), 57
Phonograph, 95
Photographs (Daguerreotypes), 77
Photography, 92
Phyfe, Duncan (1768–1854), 22, 24
Pierce, Samuel (1767–1840), 37
Piper, William T. (1881–1970), 101
Planers, 91
Plows, 74
Political items, 84
Polk, Charles Peale (1767–1822), 40
Pope Manufacturing Company, 115
Porcelain, 43, 45, 46, 47
Post, Wiley (1900–35), 127
Pottery, *16*, 17, *42*, 43, 44, 67, 80, *81*, 137

Potts, Superintendent W. L., 112
Prang, Louis (1824–1909), 141
Prints, 76, *81*, 123, 138, 140, 141
Printing, 92, 93, 94
Printing presses, 93
Prior, William M. (1806–73), 57
"Profile of the Carriage of
    George Washington," 138
Putnam Machine Company, 91

Q
Quadricycle, *2*, *142*, 143

R
Radio, 95, 98, 130
Railroads, 83, 124, *125*
Ramage, John (c. 1748–1802), 39
Ranges, 79
Raymond, S. W., 112
Read, Deborah (d. 1773), 62
Reapers, 65
Reber, John (1857–1938), 54
Remich, Christian (b. 1726; active 1768),
    140
Remington, Frederic (1861–1909), 40
Remington Arms Company, 93
Renshaw, Thomas (working 1815), 22
Revere, Paul (1735–1818), 32, 37, 140, 141
Richardson, A., Bootery, 60
Richardson, Joseph 1711–84, 32
Rip Van Winkle (play), 135
Rogers, John (1829–1904), 40
Rogers, Nathaniel (1788–1844), 39
Rogers Locomotive Works, 124
Rolls-Royce automobiles, 106, 108
Roman Bronze Works, 40
Roosevelt, Franklin D. (1882–1945), 47, 110
Roosevelt, Theodore (1858–1919), 119
Roper, Sylvester H. (d. 1896), 119
Roper Steam Carriage, 119
Routson, S. (working 1835–1886), 80
Ruef, Arnold and Peter (working c. 1880),
    57
Rush holders, 80
Rust, Samuel, 93

S
Sargent, Elmer P., 118
Schimmel, Wilhelm (1817–1890), 54
"Schoolroom Progress, U.S.A.," 136
Sculpture, 40, *41*, 54, *55*, *56*, 57, 61, 113
Sears Motor Buggy, 104
Secretary House, 141
Selden, George (1846–1932), 102
"Selected Treasures of the Henry Ford
    Museum," 130, *131*
Seneca John, *56*, 57
Sèvres porcelain, 46
Sewing machines, 79
Shaker communal society, *28*, *29*, 31
Shallenberger, 97
Shallus, Francis (1774–1821), 34

150

Shearman, Robert (working 1768–1804), 31
Shenandoah (play), 135
Sheraton, Thomas (1751–1804), 20
Sherman, Major E., 93
Sholes-Glidden Patent, 93
Sibley Lumber Company, 117
Sikorsky, Igor (1889–   ), 127
Silver, 32, *33, 34*
Singer Sewing Machine, 79
Smith, I., and Stonesifer, J., patent, 83
Smith, S., & Sons, 113
Society of the Cincinnati, 46
Speaker's Chair, Independence Hall, 10
Special events, *4, 5, 6, 7,* 129, 130, *131,* 134, 135
Special exhibitions, 62, *63, 128,* 129, 130, *131,* 132, 136
"Sports Car Show," 129
Sprite (catboat), 123
Stanton, Edwin (1814–69), 40, *41*
Steam engines, 77, 87
Stebbins, Edwin, & Co., 34
Stiegel, "Baron" Henry William (1729–85), 34
Streetcars, 101, 124
Street of Shops, *52,* 54, *55,* 58, 60, 61, 62, *67, 68, 69,* 70
Stuart, Gilbert (1755–1828), 39
Stutz automobiles, 108, *109*
Sully, Thomas (1783–1872), 39
Sun-and-Planet engine, 87
Superior Company, 75
Swope, Zuriel (working 1860), 83

T
Taft, Caleb, Blacksmith Shop, 54
"Talking Box to Telstar," 130
Taylor, Zachary (1784–1850), 93
Telegraphy, 92, *94,* 95, 98
Telephone, 98
Television, 98, *99*
Terry, Eli (1772–1852), 31
Textiles, 62, *63,* 64, *65*
Theater, 134
Theater Arts Department, 135
Theus, Jeremiah (c. 1719–74), 39
Thomas Flyer touring automobile, 104
Threshing machines, 76, 77
Tice, I. (working c. 1820), 74
Tiffany, Louis Comfort (1848–1933), 51
Tilton & Sleeper, 83
Traction engines, 77
Tractors, 77, 117
Traffic signals, 112
Transportation, 6, *100–127*
Treadway, Amos (1738–1814), 37
Trott, Benjamin (c. 1790–c. 1841), 39
Trucks, 101, 117
Truman, Harry S. (1884–   ), 47, 110, 111
Tucker, William Ellis, Factory, 45
Twain, Mark (1835–1910), 93

Typewriters, 93

U
Under the Gaslight (play), 135
U.S. Pottery Company, 45

V
Van Keuren, Isaac, 17
Van Rensselaer, Stephen (d. 1786), 34
Vought-Sikorsky Helicopter, 127

W
Wagons, 101, 116, 117
Waltham Manufacturing Company, 115
Ward, Ambrose (1735–1809), 35
Warner, Sarah Furman, 64
Washing machines, 79
Washington, George (1732–1799), 14, 20, *21,* 40, *41,* 62, *63,* 70, 138
Washington, Martha (1732–1802), 46
Washington, Mary Ball (1706–89), 14
Washington Printing Press, 93
Washtubs, 79
Water refractors, 80, *81*
Watson, John (1685–1768), 39, 138
Watt, James (1736–1819), 87
Weathervanes, 59, 120
Weaving, 137
Wedgwood, 20, *21*
Westinghouse, 97
West Newbury Volunteer Engine Co. No. 2, 121
West Point Foundry, 123
Whale oil lamps, 83
Whalen, Grover (1886–   ), 145
White, John, 80
White House, 46
Whitmore, Jacob (1736–1825), 37
Whitworth, Joseph (1803–87), 91
Wightman, I. M., 96
Will, William (1764–98), 59
Willard, Aaron (1757–1844), 31
Willard, Simon (1753–1848), 31
Wilson, Mrs. Woodrow (1872–1961), 46
Wilson, Woodrow (1856–1924), 47
Windmill End Station, 88
Winnowing basket, 76
Winthrop family, 43
Wollaston, John (working 1749–67), 39
Wood, David (1766–c. 1850), 31
Wright, Orville (1867–1912), 101, 127
Wright, Wilbur (1871–1948), 101, 127
Wright homestead, 141

Y
Young, B. S., 31
Young, Owen D., 8

Z
Zoarite, 28, 29